Test Prep

Grade 8

Test Preparation for:

Reading
Language
Math

Program Authors:
Dale Foreman
Alan C. Cohen
Jerome D. Kaplan
Ruth Mitchell

Table of Contents

Send all inquiries to:
McGraw-Hill Children's Publishing
8787 Orion Place
Columbus, OH 43240-4027

1-56189-758-2

1 2 3 4 5 6 7 8 9 10 DBH 05 04 03 02 01

Test Prep

The Program That Teaches Test-Taking Achievement

For over two decades, McGraw-Hill has helped students perform their best when taking standardized achievement tests. Over the years, we have identified the skills and strategies that students need to master the challenges of taking a standardized test. Becoming familiar with the test-taking experience can help ensure your child's success.

Test Prep covers all test skill areas

Test Prep contains the subject areas that are represented in the five major standardized tests. *Test Prep* will help your child prepare for the following tests:

- California Achievement Tests® (CAT/5)
- Comprehensive Tests of Basic Skills (CTBS/4)
- Iowa Tests of Basic Skills® (ITBS, Form K)
- Metropolitan Achievement Test (MAT/7)
- Stanford Achievement Test(SAT/9)

Test Prep provides strategies for success

Many students need special support when preparing to take a standardized test. *Test Prep* gives your child the opportunity to practice and become familiar with:

- General test content
- The test format
- Listening and following standard directions
- Working in structured settings
- Maintaining a silent, sustained effort
- Using test-taking strategies

Test Prep is comprehensive

Test Prep Provides a complete presentation of the types of skills covered in standardized tests in a variety of formats. These formats are similar to those your child will encounter when testing. The subject areas covered in this book include:

- Reading
- Language
- Math

Test Prep gives students the practice they need

Each student lesson provides several components that help develop test-taking skills:

- An **Example,** with directions and sample test items
- A **Tips** feature, that give test-taking strategies
- A **Practice** section, to help students practice answering questions in each test format

Each book gives focused test practice that builds confidence:

- A **Test Yourself** lesson for each unit gives students the opportunity to apply what they have learned in the unit
- A **Test Practice** section gives students the experience of a longer test-like situation.
- A **Progress Chart** for students to note and record their own progress.

Test Prep is the first and most successful program ever developed to help students become familiar with the test-taking experience. *Test Prep* can help to build self-confidence, reduce test anxiety, and provide the opportunity for students to successfully show what they have learned.

A Message to Parents and Teachers:

- **Standardized tests: the yardstick for your child's future**

  Standardized testing is one of the cornerstones of American education. From its beginning in the early part of this century, standardized testing has gradually become the yardstick by which student performance is judged. For better or worse, your child's future will be determined in great part by how well he or she performs on the standardized test used by your school district.

- **Even good students can have trouble with testing**

  In general, standardized tests are well designed and carefully developed to assess students' abilities in a consistent and balanced manner. However, there are many factors that can hinder the performance of an individual student when testing. These might include test anxiety, unfamiliarity with the test's format, or failure to understand the directions.

  In addition, it is rare that students are taught all of the material that appears on a standardized test. This is because the curriculum of most schools does not directly match the content of the standardized test. There will certainly be overlap between what your child learns in school and how he or she is tested, but some materials will probably be unfamiliar.

- **Ready to Test will lend a helping hand**

  It is because of the shortcomings of the standardized testing process that *Test Prep* was developed. The lessons in the book were created after a careful analysis of the most popular achievement tests. The items, while different from those on the tests, reflect the types of material that your child will encounter when testing. Students who use *Test Prep* will also become familiar with the format of the most popular achievement tests. This learning experience will reduce anxiety and give your child the opportunity to do his or her best on the next standardized test.

We urge you to review with your child the Message to Students and the feature "How to Use This Book" on pages 7-8. The information on these pages will help your child to use this book and develop important test-taking skills. We are confident that following the recommendations in this book will help your child to earn a test score that accurately reflects his or her true ability.

A Message to Students:

Frequently in school you will be asked to take a standardized achievement test. This test will show how much you know compared to other students in your grade. Your score on a standardized achievement test will help your teachers plan your education. It will also give you and your parents an idea of what your learning strengths and weaknesses are.

This book will help you do your best on a standardized achievement test. It will show you what to expect on the test and will give you a chance to practice important reading and test-taking skills. Here are some suggestions you can follow to make the best use of *Test Prep*.

Plan for success

- You'll do your best if you begin studying and do one or two lessons in this book each week. If you only have a little bit of time before a test is given, you can do one or two lessons each day.
- Study a little bit at a time, no more than 30 minutes a day. If you can, choose the same time each day to study in a quiet place.
- Keep a record of your score on each lesson. The charts on pp. 154–156 of this book will help you do this.

On the day of the test . . .

- Get a good night's sleep the night before the test. Have a light breakfast and lunch to keep from feeling drowsy during the test.
- Use the tips you learned in *Test Prep*. The most important tips are to skip difficult items, take the best guess when you're unsure of the answer, and try all the items.
- Don't worry if you are a little nervous when you take an achievement test. This is a natural feeling and may even help you stay alert.

How to Use This Book

1 Getting Started

Read the directions carefully.

Do the Sample item(s).

Read the Tip(s).

2 Practice

Complete the Practice items.

Continue working until you reach a Stop sign.

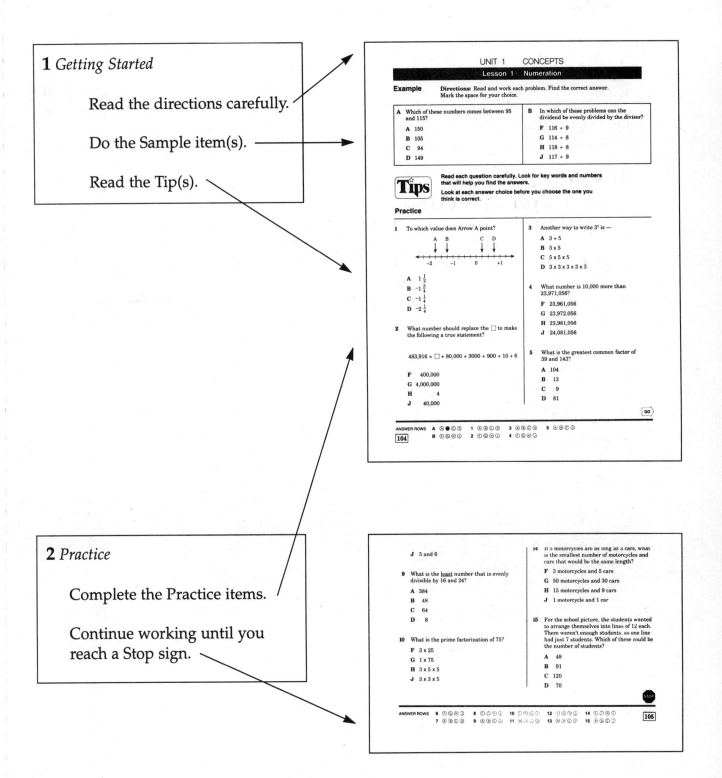

UNIT 1   CONCEPTS
Lesson 1 · Numeration

Example   Directions: Read and work each problem. Find the correct answer. Mark the space for your choice.

A Which of these numbers comes between 95 and 115?

A 150
B 105
C 94
D 149

B In which of these problems can the dividend be evenly divided by the divisor?

F 116 ÷ 9
G 114 ÷ 8
H 118 ÷ 8
J 117 ÷ 9

Tips   Read each question carefully. Look for key words and numbers that will help you find the answers.
Look at each answer choice before you choose the one you think is correct.

Practice

1 To which value does Arrow A point?

A $1\frac{1}{2}$
B $-1\frac{3}{4}$
C $-1\frac{1}{4}$
D $-2\frac{1}{4}$

2 What number should replace the □ to make the following a true statement?

483,916 = □ + 80,000 + 3000 + 900 + 10 + 6

F   400,000
G 4,000,000
H   4
J   40,000

3 Another way to write 3^5 is —

A 3 + 5
B 3 x 5
C 5 x 5 x 5
D 3 x 3 x 3 x 3 x 3

4 What number is 10,000 more than 23,971,056?

F 23,961,056
G 23,972,056
H 23,981,056
J 24,081,056

5 What is the greatest common factor of 39 and 143?

A 104
B   13
C   9
D   81

GO

ANSWER ROWS A ⓐ●©ⓓ 1 ⓐⓑ©ⓓ 3 ⓐⓑ©ⓓ 5 ⓐⓑ©ⓓ
104   B ⒡ⓖⓗ① 2 ⒡ⓖⓗ① 4 ⒡ⓖⓗ①

J 5 and 6

9 What is the least number that is evenly divisible by 16 and 24?

A 384
B   48
C   64
D   8

10 What is the prime factorization of 75?

F 3 x 25
G 1 x 75
H 3 x 5 x 5
J 3 x 3 x 5

14 If 5 motorcycles are as long as 3 cars, what is the smallest number of motorcycles and cars that would be the same length?

F 3 motorcycles and 5 cars
G 50 motorcycles and 30 cars
H 15 motorcycles and 9 cars
J 1 motorcycle and 1 car

15 For the school picture, the students wanted to arrange themselves into lines of 12 each. There weren't enough students, so one line had just 7 students. Which of these could be the number of students?

A   48
B   91
C 120
D   70

STOP

ANSWER ROWS 6 ⒡ⓖⓗ① 8 ⒡ⓖⓗ① 10 ⒡ⓖⓗ① 12 ⒡ⓖⓗ① 14 ⒡ⓖⓗ①
7 ⓐⓑ©ⓓ 9 ⓐⓑ©ⓓ 11 ⓐⓑ©ⓓ 13 ⓐⓑ©ⓓ 15 ⓐⓑ©ⓓ   105

3 *Check It Out*

Check your answers by turning to the Answer Key at the back of the book.

Keep track of how you're doing by marking the number right on the Progress Charts on pages 154-156.

Mark the lesson you completed on the table of contents for each section.

Answer Keys

Reading

Unit 1, Vocabulary

Lesson 1
A C
B F
1 A
2 J
3 B
4 H
5 D
6 F
7 B
8 H

Lesson 2
A D
B H
1 D
2 G
3 A
4 C
5 G
6 D
7 D

Lesson 3
A C
B F
1 B
2 F
3 D
4 D
5 D
6 H
7 A
8 G

Lesson 4
A D
B F
1 B
2 F
3 D
4 H
5 A

Lesson 5
A B
B J
1 B
2 F
3 C
4 J
5 A
6 H

Lesson 6
A C
B G
1 A
2 G
3 D
4 J
5 A

Lesson 7
E1 D
E2 F
1 C
2 F
3 B
4 J
5 B
6 F
7 D
8 H
9 C
10 B
11 D
12 F
13 B
14 G
15 C
16 J
17 A
18 H
19 B
20 F
21 D
22 F
23 C
24 F
25 B
26 G
27 D
28 H
29 C
30 F
31 C
32 G
33 B
34 J

Unit 2, Reading Comprehension

Lesson 8
A D
1 C
2 J
3 A

Lesson 9
A B
1 B
2 F
3 D
4 H
5 D
6 H
7 A
8 J
9 A
10 J
11 B
12 J
13 B

Lesson 10
A B
1 D
2 G
3 A
4 G
5 C
6 H
7 A
8 G
9 D
10 F
11 B
12 H
13 A
14 J
15 B
16 F
17 C
18 G
19 D
20 F
21 B
22 J

Lesson 11
E1 C
1 A
2 J
3 A
4 J
5 C
6 G
7 C
8 J
9 B
10 F
11 C
12 J
13 B
14 F
15 C
16 F
17 B
18 J
19 A
20 J
21 B
22 H
23 C
24 A
25 A
26 J
27 B
28 G
29 A
30 H
31 B
32 H
33 A

Unit 3, Test Practice
Part 1
E1 D
E2 H
1 C
2 G
3 C
4 F
5 B
6 J
7 A
8 H
9 A
10 J

Reading Progress Chart

Circle your score for each lesson. Connect your scores to see how well you are doing.

Unit 1							Unit 2			
Lesson 1	Lesson 2	Lesson 3	Lesson 4	Lesson 5	Lesson 6	Lesson 7	Lesson 8	Lesson 9	Lesson 10	Lesson 11

(Progress chart with score columns: Lesson 1: 8,7,6,5,4,3,2,1; Lesson 2: 7,6,5,4,3,2,1; Lesson 3: 8,7,6,5,4,3,2,1; Lesson 4: 5,4,3,2,1; Lesson 5: 6,5,4,3,2,1; Lesson 6: 5,4,3,2,1; Lesson 7: 34–1; Lesson 8: 3,2,1; Lesson 9: 13–1; Lesson 10: 22–1; Lesson 11: 33–1)

Table of Contents
Reading

Skills

Reading

VOCABULARY

Identifying synonyms
Identifying words with similar meanings
Identifying antonyms
Identifying multi-meaning words

Identifying words in paragraph context
Identifying word meaning from a clue
Identifying words from a defining statement

READING COMPREHENSION

Recognizing story structures
Differentiating between fact and opinion
Understanding literary devices
Identifying story genres
Recognizing details
Understanding events
Drawing conclusions
Applying story information
Deriving word or phrase meaning
Understanding characters

Sequencing ideas
Making inferences
Making comparisons
Generalizing from story information
Identifying strategic reading techniques
Choosing the best title for a story
Using a story web
Understanding the author's purpose
Understanding feelings
Understanding the main idea

Language

LANGUAGE MECHANICS

Identifying the need for punctuation marks
(period, question marks, exclamation
point, quotation marks, apostrophe,
comma, colon, semicolon,) in sentences

Identifying the need for capital letters and
punctuation marks in printed text

LANGUAGE EXPRESSION

Identifying the correct forms of verbs,
adverbs, adjectives, and pronouns
Identifying the subject of a sentence
Combining sentences
Identifying redundant sentences
Identifying the correct sentence to complete
a paragraph
Sequencing sentences within a paragraph
Identifying run-on sentences

Recognizing double negatives
Identifying incorrectly used words or phrases
Identifying the predicate of a sentence
Identifying correctly formed sentences
Identifying sentences that do not fit in a
paragraph
Choosing the right paragraph for a given
purpose

SPELLING

Identifying correctly spelled words

Identifying incorrectly spelled words

STUDY SKILLS

Taking notes
Understanding a chart
Understanding the use of reference methods
Choosing an appropriate topic
Understanding a table of contents
Alphabetizing words

Using a map
Completing an application
Using a thesaurus
Identifying reference sources
Identifying a search topic

Math

COMPUTATION

Adding whole numbers, integers, decimals, and fractions

Subtracting whole numbers, decimals, and fractions

Multiplying whole numbers, integers, decimals, and fractions

Dividing whole numbers, integers, decimals, and fractions

CONCEPTS

Using expanded notation

Comparing and ordering whole numbers and integers

Finding multiples

Associating numerals and number words

Understanding place value

Understanding number sentences

Rounding

Identifying fractional parts

Comparing and ordering fractions and decimals

Reducing fractions

Converting among decimals, fractions, and percents

Finding square roots

Using exponents and exponential notation

Factoring numbers and finding the greatest common factor

Recognizing prime and composite numbers

Recognizing numeric patterns

Using operational symbols and properties

Estimating

Understanding decimal place value

Recognizing equivalent fractions and reciprocals

Identifying the lowest common denominator

Renaming fractions and decimals

Using a number line with fractions and decimals

APPLICATIONS

Understanding congruence and transformations

Finding perimeter, area, and volume

Understanding points, lines, segments and angles, and their characteristics

Understanding time concepts

Reading a thermometer

Understanding bar, line, and circle graphs

Solving oral and written word problems

Understanding probability, averages, and combinations

Formulating simple number sentences

Understanding inequalities

Recognizing plane and solid figures and their characteristics

Recognizing value of money and money notation

Using standard and metric units of measurement

Estimating weight and size

Understanding tables and charts

Identifying information needed to solve a problem

Understanding ratio and proportion

Using a coordinate graph

Solving simple equations

Strategies

Listening carefully

Following group directions

Adjusting to a structured setting

Utilizing test formats

Maintaining a silent, sustained effort

Locating questions and answer choices

Managing time effectively

Considering every answer choice

Noting the lettering of answer choices

Recalling word meanings

Taking the best guess when unsure of the answer

Skipping difficult items and returning to them later

Identifying the best test-taking strategy

Working methodically

Comparing answer choices

Eliminating answer choices

Rereading questions

Referring to a passage to find the correct answer

Using logic

Recalling the elements of a correctly formed sentence

Locating the correct answer

Identifying and using key words, figures, and numbers

Recalling the elements of a correctly formed paragraph

Following written directions

Taking the best guess

Substituting answer choices

Marking the right answer as soon as it is found

Understanding unusual item formats

Following complex directions

Trying out answer choices

Using context to find the answer

Inferring word meaning from sentence context

Converting problems to a workable format

Staying with the first answer

Previewing items

Responding to items according to difficulty

Finding the answer without computing

Analyzing questions

Identifying and using key words to find the answer

Skimming a passage

Referring to a passage to answer questions

Indicating that the correct answer is not given

Subvocalizing answer choices

Indicating that an item has no mistakes

Reasoning from facts and evidence

Avoiding overanalysis of answer choices

Referring to a reference source

Checking answers by the opposite operation

Performing the correct operation

Reworking a problem

Computing carefully

Using answer choices as a clue to finding the right answer

Checking answers

Table of Contents
Reading

UNIT 1   VOCABULARY

Lesson 1   Synonyms

Examples   **Directions:** Read each item. Choose the word that means the same or about the same as the underlined word.

A **negotiate** a deal	**B** To **alternate** goals is to —
A cancel	F switch
B investigate	G achieve
C arrange *(circled)*	H reinforce
D question	J ignore

 Read each question and the answer choices carefully. Make sure the space you darken in the answer rows matches the question on which you are working.

Practice

1 **discontinue** the newspaper

   A cancel
   B buy
   C enjoy
   D lose

2 great **impact**

   F inspection
   G friendship
   H investment
   J influence

3 **generate** support

   A afford
   B create
   C appreciate
   D avoid

4 **endure** hardships

   F reject
   G reduce
   H tolerate
   J increase

5 To **reside** nearby is to —

   A build
   B visit
   C move
   D live

6 A terrible **stench** —

   F odor
   G roar
   H sound
   J accident

7 Great **turmoil** —

   A concern
   B disorder
   C mountain
   D calm

8 **Trivial** payments are —

   F huge
   G quick
   H small
   J slow

STOP

Examples   **Directions:** Read each item. Choose the answer that means the same or about the same as the underlined word.

A **Scorn** their help **A** ask for **B** reject with contempt **C** accept with joy **D** worry about	**B** Toshi is a **competent** worker. To be **competent** is to be — **F** inadequate **G** busy **H** capable **J** quiet

 If you aren't sure which answer is correct, take your best guess.

Practice

1 Avoid **misfortune**

  A good luck
  B a large amount of money
  C a small amount of money
  D bad luck

2 Do something **manually**

  F by computer
  G by hand
  H by machine
  J by command

3 **Cherish** a memory

  A hold dear
  B think badly of
  C recall
  D forget

4 We set up **partitions** in the room.

  F video equipment
  G rows of chairs
  H dividing walls
  J exhibition booths

5 One **component** hasn't arrived yet.

  Component means —

  A visitor
  B team
  C part
  D competitor

6 The large horse was **docile**.

  Docile means —

  F energetic
  G easy to manage
  H hard to ride
  J aggressive

7 The schedule you are proposing seems **feasible**.

  Feasible means —

  A impossible
  B difficult
  C enjoyable
  D reasonable

STOP

ANSWER ROWS   **A** Ⓐ Ⓑ Ⓒ Ⓓ   **1** Ⓐ Ⓑ Ⓒ Ⓓ   **3** Ⓐ Ⓑ Ⓒ Ⓓ   **5** Ⓐ Ⓑ Ⓒ Ⓓ   **7** Ⓐ Ⓑ Ⓒ Ⓓ
                 B Ⓕ Ⓖ Ⓗ Ⓙ   **2** Ⓕ Ⓖ Ⓗ Ⓙ   **4** Ⓕ Ⓖ Ⓗ Ⓙ   **6** Ⓕ Ⓖ Ⓗ Ⓙ

Examples

Directions: Read each item. Choose the answer that means the opposite of the underlined word.

A luscious fruit **A** sweet and juicy **B** ready to eat **C** tasteless and dry **D** pretty to look at	**B a voluntary action** **F** required **G** sudden **H** friendly **J** angry

 Skip difficult items and come back to them later. If you are still not sure of the right answer, eliminate choices you know are wrong and then take your best guess from the remaining answers.

Practice

1 gallant knights

   A brave
   B cowardly
   C armed
   D elegant

2 bisect something

   F put together
   G cut in half
   H discover
   J replace

3 genuine leather

   A beautiful
   B inexpensive
   C real
   D fake

4 reveal the truth

   F suspect
   G doubt
   H keep hidden
   J make known

5 become belligerent

   A angry
   B warlike
   C competitive
   D peaceful

6 was prohibited

   F forbidden
   G difficult
   H allowed
   J simple

7 appear unkempt

   A neat
   B lazy
   C messy
   D tired

8 feel malice

   F concern
   G kindness
   H satisfied
   J anger

STOP

Examples   **Directions:** Read each item. Choose the answer you think is correct.

A | Can you page Dr. Henderson? |

In which sentence does the word page mean the same thing as in the sentence above?

A   Which page are you reading?

B   The page held the knight's lance.

C   I like to page through catalogs.

D   Page me when you need a ride home.

Choose the word that fits best in both sentences.

B   The _____ was locked at five o'clock.

Sandy was _____ at second base.

F   safe

G   door

H   out

J   chest

Skim the items. Answer the easiest items first. Then go back and do the more difficult items.

Use context to find the best answer.

Practice

1 | A command is wrong in this software. |

In which sentence does the word command mean the same thing as in the sentence above?

A   The king will command your presence.

B   Each command tells the computer to do a different thing.

C   The general is in command here.

D   She will command respect everywhere.

2 | Close the flap, then tape the box. |

In which sentence does the word flap mean the same thing as in the sentence above?

F   The flap with the address should be on the outside.

G   The huge bird began to flap its wings.

H   Her story made quite a flap.

J   The shutter began to flap against the house when the wind picked up.

3   The bell will _____ at noon.

Gloria lost her _____ in the kitchen.

A   sound

B   glove

C   pen

D   ring

4   The runner began to _____ .

That _____ is still in good shape.

F   sweat

G   car

H   tire

J   turn

5   This is a very _____ problem.

The apartment _____ has a pool.

A   complex

B   difficult

C   building

D   simple

Lesson 5   Words in Context

Examples   **Directions:** Read the paragraph. Find the word below the paragraph that fits best in each blank.

Buying a new car is more _____**(A)**_____ than you might think. You have to ___**(B)**___ which car you want and then shop for the best price. Most people then have to borrow money from a bank to pay for the new car.

A A partial
    B involved
    C unlikely
    D meaningful

B F deny
    G socialize
    H furnish
    J determine

 **Tips**   Skim the paragraph. Use its meaning to find the right answer. If necessary, try substituting each answer choice in the blank.

Practice

The trucker was _____**(1)**_____ of the accident ahead by a call on her radio. Markie began to ___**(2)**___ , and as she approached the scene, she saw that it looked pretty bad. Several cars had already stopped at the wreck, so she ___**(3)**___ that the injured passengers were being helped. Markie pulled on to the ___**(4)**___ of the road about one hundred yards ahead of the accident, put her flashers on, and set ___**(5)**___ flares along the road. She grabbed her first-aid kit from the truck and ___**(6)**___ up to the wreck.

1 A alarmed
   B informed
   C suspicious
   D involved

2 F decelerate
   G refrain
   H extinguish
   J rescind

3 A denied
   B resented
   C concluded
   D compounded

4 F intersection
   G instinct
   H proximity
   J shoulder

5 A caution
   B inhibited
   C isolated
   D incidental

6 F bantered
   G unweighted
   H bolted
   J swindled

STOP

Examples   **Directions:** Read each question. Fill in the circle for the answer
you think is correct.

A   Which of these words probably comes
    from the Old Icelandic word *gapa*
    meaning *a mouth that is opened wide*?

    A   gain
    B   gourd
    C   gape
    D   grate

B   Raymond was _____ when he
    learned his bike was missing.

    Which of these words means Raymond
    was bothered very much?

    F   angry
    G   distraught
    H   confused
    J   relaxed

Stay with the first answer choice. Change it only if you are sure it
is wrong and another answer is better.

Practice

1   Which of these words probably comes
    from the Middle English word *muflein*
    meaning *wrapped up*?

    A   muffled
    B   mottled
    C   mounted
    D   molted

2   Which of these words probably comes
    from the Latin word *quaerere* meaning
    to seek?

    F   quaint
    G   quest
    H   quell
    J   quince

3   Which of these words probably comes
    from the Middle English word *couchen*
    meaning *to lie down*?

    A   cloud
    B   crowd
    C   catch
    D   crouch

4   The judges tried to make an _____
    decision in the science contest.

    Which of these words means the
    decision was fair?

    F   influential
    G   irresponsible
    H   offensive
    J   impartial

5   Gina felt _____ after staying up late
    to watch the eclipse.

    Which of these words means Gina
    didn't have much energy?

    A   sluggish
    B   fictitious
    C   ambitious
    D   hopeless

STOP

ANSWER ROWS   A Ⓐ Ⓑ Ⓒ Ⓓ   1 Ⓐ Ⓑ Ⓒ Ⓓ   3 Ⓐ Ⓑ Ⓒ Ⓓ   5 Ⓐ Ⓑ Ⓒ Ⓓ
              B Ⓕ Ⓖ Ⓗ Ⓙ   2 Ⓕ Ⓖ Ⓗ Ⓙ   4 Ⓕ Ⓖ Ⓗ Ⓙ

Example

Directions: For E1, find the word that means the same or about the same as the underlined word in the phrase. For E2, read the question. Mark the answer you think is correct.

E1　be obliged to attend

A　asked
B　happy
C　unhappy
D　required

E2　Which of these probably comes from the Middle English word *faltre* meaning *to be uncertain*?

F　falter
G　flatten
H　father
J　folder

For numbers 1-8, find the word or words that mean the same or almost the same as the underlined word.

1　a fast tempo

A　song
B　dance
C　pace
D　car

2　a tract of land

F　region
G　deed
H　purchase
J　sale

3　massive rocks

A　small
B　huge
C　beautiful
D　ancient

4　plot a revolution

F　end
G　join
H　lose
J　plan

5　A tyrant is —

A　a fair leader
B　an unjust ruler
C　a police officer
D　an enemy

6　A long reign is a —

F　period of rule
G　strike
H　time of famine
G　relationship

7　An unusual specimen is a —

A　jungle animal
B　event
C　sound
D　scientific sample

8　Crucial evidence is —

F　useless
G　medical
H　important
J　hidden

GO

9 Felicia made an <u>impartial</u> decision.

<u>Impartial</u> means —

A hasty
B emotional
C fair
D biased

10 Did you <u>inquire</u> about the cost?

To <u>inquire</u> is to —

F ask
G talk
H argue
J bargain

11 Abdul wrote his notes on the <u>margin</u> of the paper.

<u>Margin</u> means —

A middle
B back
C front
D edge

12 Did Paula <u>regret</u> going to the meeting?

To <u>regret</u> is to feel —

F sorry about
G good about
H undecided about
J concerned about

13 The company's new <u>slogan</u> is exciting.

A <u>slogan</u> is a —

A product
B saying
C building
D plan

For numbers 14-19, find the word that means the opposite of the underlined word.

14 <u>alert</u> sentry

F attentive
G inattentive
H frightened
J lonely

15 <u>inaccurate</u> statement

A long
B wrong
C correct
D hopeful

16 <u>versatile</u> tool

F expensive
G having many uses
H inexpensive
J having only one use

17 should <u>encounter</u>

A avoid
B attract
C attribute
D isolate

18 <u>erratic</u> flight

F swift
G incredible
H straight
J minimal

19 <u>intense</u> feelings

A empty
B weak
C strong
D irate

GO

ANSWER ROWS   **9** (A)(B)(C)(D)   **11** (A)(B)(C)(D)   **13** (A)(B)(C)(D)   **15** (A)(B)(C)(D)   **17** (A)(B)(C)(D)   **19** (A)(B)(C)(D)
                10 (F)(G)(H)(J)   **12** (F)(G)(H)(J)   **14** (F)(G)(H)(J)   **16** (F)(G)(H)(J)   **18** (F)(G)(H)(J)

For numbers 20-23, choose the word that correctly completes <u>both</u> sentences.

20 We heard a _____ sound from the room above us.

It was so hot I was sure I would _____ while we stood in line.

  F faint
  G quiet
  H collapse
  J dim

21 The Johnsons are _____ to the Murrays who live next door to us.

When Karen _____ her story, she presented all the details.

  A associated
  B recited
  C disclosed
  D related

22 The knight wore a coat of _____ to protect him in battle.

We can _____ the package today and hope it arrives on time.

  F mail
  G ship
  H leather
  J send

23 You will have to complete this form to _____ for the job.

Be careful when you _____ the medicine to the burned area.

  A interview
  B rub
  C apply
  D compete

24 | The singers did a <u>fine</u> job.

In which sentence does the word <u>fine</u> mean the same thing as in the sentence above?

  F We enjoyed a <u>fine</u> dinner at a small restaurant.
  G The <u>fine</u> for speeding is $50.
  H The <u>fine</u> sand blew into the tent.
  J There are many <u>fine</u> details in this painting.

25 | The <u>title</u> of this story doesn't match what <u>it</u> is about.

In which sentence does the word <u>title</u> mean the same thing as in the sentence above?

  A There seems to be some confusion about the <u>title</u> to the house.
  B I forget the <u>title</u>, but the movie was about a survivor of a shipwreck.
  C His <u>title</u> was the Duke of York.
  D She held the tennis <u>title</u> for seven years.

26 | Will she be able to <u>lead</u> the team?

In which sentence does the word <u>lead</u> mean the same thing as in the sentence above?

  F The horse's <u>lead</u> was dragging on the ground.
  G The best way to <u>lead</u> is by example.
  H The <u>lead</u> singer thanked the others in his group.
  J Our <u>lead</u> was down to two runs.

GO

27 Which of these words probably comes from the Scandinavian word *bangla* meaning *to work ineffectively*?

A bugle
B bundle
C bridle
D bungle

28 Which of these words probably comes from the Middle English word *desolatus* meaning *forsaken*?

F deploy
G deny
H desolate
J disintegrate

29 We were able to _____ the cold because we had the right clothes.

Which of these words means we were able to put up with the cold?

A tedious
B satiate
C tolerate
D impend

30 The surface of the statue had been _____ by the weather.

Which of these words means the surface of the statue had been eaten away?

F corroded
G corroborated
H deflected
J harried

Read the paragraph. Find the word below the paragraph that fits best in each numbered blank.

Margita ____(31)____ thought that her brother's idea to open a lemonade stand was ____(32)____ . She went along with the idea because she wanted to ____(33)____ him. Sancho was only twelve, but he had big ideas about going into business. They obtained a license from the town clerk, built a pushcart, and parked their cart near the courthouse. By the end of the summer, Margita had ____(34)____ her position completely. She and Sancho had earned more than $5,000.

31 A moderately
   B incessantly
   C initially
   D desperately

32 F adroit
   G absurd
   H dependable
   J optimistic

33 A berate
   B encourage
   C dismay
   D insinuate

34 F solidified
   G partaken
   H deteriorated
   J reversed

21

STOP

ANSWER ROWS   **27** Ⓐ Ⓑ Ⓒ Ⓓ   **29** Ⓐ Ⓑ Ⓒ Ⓓ   **31** Ⓐ Ⓑ Ⓒ Ⓓ   **33** Ⓐ Ⓑ Ⓒ Ⓓ
      28 Ⓕ Ⓖ Ⓗ Ⓙ   **30** Ⓕ Ⓖ Ⓗ Ⓙ   **32** Ⓕ Ⓖ Ⓗ Ⓙ   **34** Ⓕ Ⓖ Ⓗ Ⓙ   NUMBER RIGHT _____

Example

Directions: Read each item. Choose the answer you think is correct. Mark the space for your answer.

The ad in the paper was for a "driver's helper." Judy didn't know what that was, but she decided to apply. To her surprise, she got the job, and discovered it was to work on an ice truck. She rode with the driver as he made his deliveries and helped him unload the ice and fill up customers' freezers.

A   Which of these is a fact from the story?

  A   The job sounds like fun.

  B   Papers are the best place to find jobs.

  C   Loading ice is hard work.

  D   Judy got the job.

 **Tips**

Read the question, look at the answer choices, then read the question again. Choose the answer you think is right, then compare it to the question again.

Practice

Read this passage. Then do numbers 1-2.

He was a failure, at least as far as the people of Spain were concerned. He hadn't found the Cities of Gold, nor had he returned with great treasure. Francisco Coronado, had, however, explored much of the New World, and had brought the Spanish culture to a region that would eventually become the American Southwestern states.

1   Which of these is a fact expressed in the passage?

  A   Because he had not found treasure, Coronado was a failure.

  B   The Spanish culture is best suited for warm climates like the Southwest.

  C   Coronado explored a region that would become part of America.

  D   Coronado was the most successful of the Spanish explorers.

2   This passage would most likely be found in —

  F   a fiction story.

  G   a travel brochure.

  H   an adventure story.

  J   a biography.

For number 3, choose the best answer to the question.

3   Which of these probably came from a science fiction story?

  A   The children of the pioneers who had been born in space had an unusual trait.

  B   The distances between stars are so great as to be unimaginable.

  C   "Madam," the waiter whispered, "the fly is doing the backstroke."

  D   Like the other buildings in the town, the restaurant had quite a history.

 STOP

Example

Directions: Read each passage. Find the best answer to the questions that follow the passage.

Clyde and Bonnie met their friends at the Harlow Creek bridge. They had planned a picnic for Labor Day, but before the fun began, they had a job to do. They had decided to spend two hours picking up litter from around the bridge and the picnic area before they had their own picnic. They figured it was a small price to pay to enjoy a clean park.

A **After they finish their work, the young people will probably feel —**

  A tired and dejected.

  B tired and satisfied.

  C dejected and annoyed.

  D annoyed and tired.

Look for key words in the question. If you can find the same key words in the story, you will find the right answer nearby.

Practice

Read the letter below. Use it to answer the questions on the following page.

134 Fifth Street
Contentment, Texas 75444
June 15, 1996

Dear Jerry,

My family and I would like you to visit us for two weeks, starting July 3. My dad can pick you up at the airport, and he will take you back for the return trip. Since your family moved to Michigan last year, all your friends here miss you and are eager to see you again.

The annual Fourth of July town picnic, parade, and fireworks show will be spectacular, as usual. The theme this year is "The Champions of Contentment." Our class has a float that will feature the people who have won awards during the year. The band will march and play, and there will be horses and clowns. We are even having a pet beauty contest. Won't that be great?

After things settle down from that, we can go fishing in the abandoned rock quarry at the edge of town. It has been stocked with rainbow trout. Mother has promised to cook what we catch, but we have to clean the fish ourselves.

We will go to my grandfather's farm for a day or two and help him stack his hay in the barn. It will be hard work, but we can ride his horses in the hills when we are finished.

On July 11, the YMCA swim classes will hold a demonstration. I will finish my lifeguard course this summer. Of course, you'll want to be there when I "rescue" someone and then get my medal and certificate. I'll have to go to classes for a few mornings, so you will be forced to play pool, lift weights, or do something else at the Y while I am in swim classes. I am sure you won't mind that!

All of us are looking forward to your visit, and we have lots of things planned. Rest up before you come, because we will be too busy to rest much while you are here. Please let us know as soon as you can when you will arrive!

Your friend,
Joe

1   How often is the town's celebration held?

   A   Once a month
   B Once a year
   C   Once every five years
   D   This is the first one

2   Which of these is most likely to happen next?

   F   Joe will hear from Jerry.
   G   Joe will visit his grandfather.
   H Jerry will catch the next plane to Texas.
   J   Joe will get his lifeguard certificate.

3   In this letter, the word "rescue" in quotation marks means that —

   A   Joe will really save someone's life.
   B   the ceremony will have to wait until Joe rescues someone.
   C   the class will only talk about rescuing people.
   D Joe will not actually save a person but will pretend to.

4   Where will the boys ride horses?

   F   at the quarry.
   G   near the YMCA.
   H in the hills.
   J   the letter doesn't say.

5   Joe's letter suggests that he and Jerry both like —

   A   watching television and movies best.
   B   reading books and magazines.
   C   going to picnics and parties.
   D doing active things.

6   What kind of letter is this?

   F   Letter of complaint
   G   Business letter
   H Friendly letter
   J   Letter to the editor

7   In this letter, the phrase "forced to play pool or lift weights" means that —

   A   Jerry will actually enjoy doing these things.
   B   Joe hopes Jerry won't mind doing these things because they are not fun.
   C   the two boys won't be spending much time together.
   D there are some things Jerry will do even if he doesn't like them.

GO

Glaciers

In some very cold regions of the earth, the snow never melts. As more snow falls, the accumulated mass of the snowfield becomes heavy, and the weight compacts the lower level of snow to ice. Over time, glaciers form. They are masses of snow and ice that glide along the ground. These huge ice masses exist where the annual snowfall is so great it doesn't melt, such as the polar regions and in very high mountains. Glacial ice now covers about 10 percent of the earth's land area.

Snow is fluffy when it falls, but when it accumulates without melting, it becomes granular and eventually compacts into solid ice. The solid glaciers move at a speed that depends on the glacier's weight and the steepness of the slope. In steep mountains, they can move 60 feet per day. In addition, the lower levels move more than the top, and great rifts or cracks form, making glacier exploration hazardous.

There are two kinds of glaciers: valley glaciers and ice sheets. A third kind, piedmont glaciers, is a combination of the other two. Valley glaciers follow the high valleys of mountains such as the Rockies, the Cascades, or the Alps. Rocks on the underside scrape the valleys and make them wider, deeper, and U-shaped. The glacier continues moving to the warmer lowlands, where part of it melts.

An ice sheet is a broad layer of ice that spreads outward in all directions. It is usually slower moving than valley glaciers because of the flatter terrain on which it forms. A continental glacier is an ice sheet that covers most of a continent. Greenland and Antarctica are largely covered by continental glaciers. Sometimes two valley glaciers merge at a low level and fan out over a large area to form a piedmont glacier, which looks much like an ice sheet.

Pieces of a glacier at the edge of the ocean can break off and become icebergs. These huge floating chunks of ice have sunk many ships. In 1912, when the *Titanic* struck an iceberg in the Atlantic Ocean, more than 1500 lives were lost.

Glaciers shaped our land masses through erosion by gouging out and moving rocks and dirt. They also create deposits as they transport debris and drop it in new places. In the Rocky Mountains of Colorado, many of the spectacular peaks were formed by valley glaciers. This is also true of Yosemite Falls in California. The fiords and inlet harbors of Norway and Greenland were carved out by glacial sculpture. The lakes that dot the northern part of the United States were formed by the melting ends of glaciers. Glaciers are responsible for underground reservoirs of water and for mineral-rich soil in some areas.

Climate changes that have accompanied glaciers have even affected human beings' development and their migrations on the planet. During cold weather, when glaciers grew, humans moved to warmer areas. When the glaciers receded, people were able to move back and settle in northern areas.

GO

8 There is enough information in this article to show that —

  F glaciers existed long ago but are not on earth now.

  G piedmont glaciers and ice sheets do not move.

  H icebergs formed by glaciers can be very dangerous.

  J the speed of glaciers depends on how much snow there is.

9 The web shows some important ideas in the article.

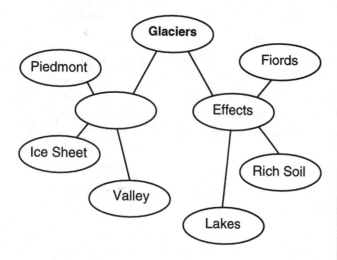

Which of these belongs in the empty space?

  A Types

  B Icebergs

  C Glacial sculpture

  D Snow to ice

10 A piedmont glacier is —

  F always near an ocean.

  G more slow moving than either a valley glacier or an ice sheet.

  H a continental glacier.

  J formed when two valley glaciers come together.

11 The principal reason that glaciers form is because —

  A the temperature of the earth is lower than before.

  B snow falls faster than it melts.

  C snow melts and then refreezes in mountain valleys.

  D icebergs accumulate near the coastline of polar regions.

12 This article was written in order to —

  F express an opinion.

  G describe a problem.

  H compare two ideas.

  J present facts.

13 The climate changes that accompanied the glaciers—

  A caused many animal species to become extinct.

  B affected humans' development and migrations.

  C increased the number of icebergs.

  D formed most of the mountain ranges.

STOP

Example   **Directions:** Read each passage. Find the best answer to each question that follows the passage.

Many people who feed birds dislike one of our feathered friends, the jay. It is large, aggressive, and noisy, often chasing other birds away from a feeder. If a group of jays comes to a feeder, they can often empty it in minutes searching for the food they like best.	**A** **The author of this story —** **A** enjoys watching jays. **B** describes jays in negative terms. **C** feels jays are good feeder visitors. **D** enjoys taking photos of birds.

 **Skim the passage, then look at the questions. Answer the easiest questions first. Then do the more difficult questions.**

Practice

What makes a hero?

Much has been said and written recently about heroes, chiefly because many people think we have too few of them. There are many different kinds of heroes, but they all seem to have two things in common. First, heroes, by their actions, reveal the great possibilities of human nature. Second, heroes can also stand the test of time, and their accomplishments will not be easily forgotten. Because of these characteristics, we need to choose our heroes carefully.

Olympic track star Jackie Joyner-Kersee, who many people believe is a hero, warns young people to be careful of making heroes of athletes. She hopes that if someone tries to imitate her, it will be because she accomplished her goals by working hard. Joyner-Kersee says that a hero should be someone who has made a difference in another person's life.

Poet Maya Angelou believes that a hero inspires people to treat others well and to be concerned about the greater good. A hero should display courtesy, courage, patience, and strength all the time. A hero should inspire others to follow their concerns with actions that improve the world, even if only in small ways.

Author Daniel Boorstin suggests that, "*Celebrities* are people who make news, but heroes are people who make history." Thus, if a person truly deserves to be called a hero, he or she will not be soon forgotten.

We all need heroes. We need to be able to look up to people who have been there, done that, and succeeded. Many times the greatest heroes are the people we deal with daily— relatives, friends, and neighbors—who have kept going when it would have been easier to give up. The parent who puts her or his family ahead of a potential athletic career, the grandparent who chooses to stay and work instead of seeking fortune, the teacher who might have made more money at another career but chose to help others—all of these people can be classified as heroes. A hero quietly and steadily sets a good example, an example that beckons others to follow it.

1   A good title for this passage is —

A "Sports Heroes"

B "There Are No More Heroes"

C "Heroes, Who Needs Them?"

D "Everyday Heroes"

2   In the selection, heroes are defined as all of these except —

F people who have made a difference in someone's life.

G people who have made a fortune at their careers.

H people who have kept going and not given up.

J people who make history and not just news.

3   There is enough information in this story to show that —

A different people have different definitions of who is a hero.

B we have fewer heroes today than we did in the past.

C it is rare when a typical person has a chance to become a hero.

D young people today really don't need heroes anymore.

4   Which words would best describe a hero?

F ...two things in common...

G ...stand the test of time...

H ...made more money...

J ...people who make news...

5   Why do people need heroes?

A To show how to make news and bring great fame

B Because most people don't know how to do the right thing

C To set a good example for them follow

D Because the world is a very different place than it was before

6   The writer probably includes the first sentence to —

F show that sports figures are heroes.

G establish the time frame for the passage.

H prepare the reader for what is to come.

J introduce the people in the passage.

7   In this passage *celebrities* are —

A people who make news.

B everyday heroes.

C athletes to be imitated.

D people who make history.

GO

Are horses our best friends?

In movies about the Old West, the cowboy often loved his horse more than he loved any human being. The two were inseparable, and the man depended on his strong companion every day. Today, machines do much of the work on a ranch, but cowboys still depend on their steeds. Many other people today use horses for recreation or keep them as pets.

The early horse, called eohippus, was about the size of a fox and lived fifty million years ago. Over the years, this little relative of the horse grew and became strong. Between ten and five thousand years ago, humans learned to tame and ride horses, and they became an important part of our history.

Genghis Khan and his warriors from Mongolia used horses to control much of Asia and Europe. Arabs developed one of the finest breeds in the world and loved their horses so much that they let them sleep in their tents. The Spanish explorers brought horses to the Americas, and when they escaped and multiplied, horses changed the lifestyles of many Native Americans forever. These Spanish horses, called mustangs, allowed Plains Indians to hunt buffalo more efficiently. They learned to ride horses with unmatched skill, and the Comanches and Apaches were said to ride as if they and the horse were one.

The mustangs also served Western settlers and cattlemen well, and both the U.S. Cavalry and Pony Express used them. They were known for their speed and endurance, and were able to withstand the harsh weather of the deserts, plains, and mountains. The mustang, with its love of freedom, has come to be a *symbol* of the American West.

The quarter horse, which was bred from the mustang, was America's first racing horse. Anyone who rides on rough mountain trails will appreciate the strength and surefootedness of the quarter horse. These beautiful animals have great stamina and speed, but are bred to run only short distances.

Thoroughbreds are the principal racers in America today, and were imported from England more than a century ago. All thoroughbreds are descendants of Arabian horses taken to England in the 1700s. Thoroughbreds are not as strong as quarter horses, but they can run faster for longer distances.

Quarter horses, thoroughbreds, Arabians, and other specialized breeds of horses are popular around the world. Even though they don't serve people in the way they did a hundred years ago, they are still used for work, for competition, and for pleasure riding. And as anyone who owns a horse will tell you, they are lovable animals that can easily find their way into your heart.

8 **Which words tell how much some people loved their horses?**

F ...they and the horse were one...

G ...they let them sleep in their tents...

H ...use horses for recreation...

J ...its love of freedom...

9 **The boxes show some of the main ideas in this passage.**

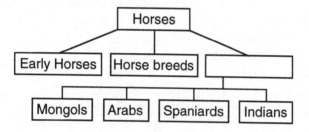

Which of these belongs in the empty box?

A How horses were used

B Racing horses

C Riding horses

D People who used horses

10 **Before Spanish explorers arrived in the Americas —**

F horses were there.

G American horses were the size of a fox.

H Native Americans rode buffalos.

J cowboys used horses.

11 **In the passage, the word *symbol* means —**

A a mathematics sign.

B a thing that stands for something else.

C a picture of a horse.

D how people learned to ride horses.

12 **The lifestyles of the American Indians changed when horses were brought to the New World because —**

F the horses were a major source of food.

G they worshipped the horses.

H they could travel and hunt better.

J Apaches and Comanches became allies.

13 **Which of these is an *opinion* stated in the passage?**

A Horses are lovable.

B Quarter horses are fast for short distances.

C Mongols used horses.

D Arabian horses came to America from England.

14 **This passage can best be described as —**

F an editorial.

G an adventure.

H a review.

J a description.

GO

Animal Attraction

Almost every major city in the world shares one attraction, a zoo. From the Philadelphia Zoological Garden, America's oldest zoo, to the one in Sydney, Australia, which most people reach by ferry, zoos are loved by tourists and residents alike.

Humans have kept animals for their enjoyment and entertainment from prehistoric times. The ancient Egyptians, Greeks, and Romans kept small zoos, but the origin of the zoo as we know it today took place during the Renaissance in sixteenth century Europe. These zoos were termed "menageries" because they were an attempt to bring together at least one of each type of animal. By the eighteenth century, there were major zoos in Vienna, Austria; Paris, France; Madrid, Spain; and London, England.

Over the past several hundred years, zoos have changed considerably. At first, they were no better than prisons for animals, with small cages and barely acceptable food. In the last fifty or so years, however, zoos have provided animals with larger and more natural habitats, better food, and opportunities for recreation and socialization. Zoos also moved from being purely entertainment to serving as research and education centers. These changes have improved life for the animals in the zoos, have helped us preserve animals in the wild, and have made visiting a zoo more enjoyable for both children and adults.

The idea that a zoo should be a menagerie is also changing. In some places, the zoo has focused on animals from a particular habitat, such as the Arizona-Sonora Desert Museum in Tucson or Ghost Ranch in northern New Mexico. In others, the emphasis is providing an "up close and personal" experience by allowing visitors to drive through areas where animals range freely in an open habitat.

Almost all zoos are owned by nonprofit organizations or municipalities such as cities or counties. They are supported by admission fees, the sale of food or merchandise in the zoo, taxes, or gifts from charitable foundations. In the United States, Canada, and most European nations, zoos belong to a professional association that conducts regular inspections to see that the animals are receiving appropriate treatment.

Many people are surprised to learn that the majority of the employees in a zoo are responsible for administration, maintaining grounds, taking tickets, selling food and merchandise, and other routine functions. The two "glamour" jobs are curator and zookeeper, and there are relatively few of these positions available in any zoo. A curator is responsible for acquiring animals, designing exhibits, supervising animal care, and performing related tasks. A zookeeper is the person visitors see bathing the elephants, feeding the lions, or making sure the rhinoceros has a stout rubbing post. In addition to these two positions, most zoos have at least one veterinarian, some technicians, and perhaps an animal researcher or two.

A modern zoo requires as much administration as a small city. Visitors see only a small part of what is involved in running a zoo. A great deal of effort must be expended to maintain the health and well-being of the animals, protect keepers who work with the animals, and create an environment that is stimulating for the animals and entertaining for visitors. All this effort seems to be paying off, however, for zoos are popular attractions year-round, and it is a rare person indeed who doesn't enjoy spending a day at a zoo.

GO

15 A menagerie would have —

  A many examples of the same animal.

  B examples of many different animals.

  C animals in a natural setting.

  D animals in cramped cages.

16 What is a major difference between modern zoos and those of a hundred years ago?

  F Animals are treated better today.

  G Animals are treated worse today.

  H Cages were larger a hundred years ago.

  J Most zoos are in large cities today.

17 In the third paragraph, what does the word "socialization" mean?

  A To exercise

  B To eat natural foods

  C To spend time together in natural groups

  D To learn more about keepers and people who visit a zoo

18 What is a "glamour" job?

  F One that requires the worker to be attractive

  G One that seems like fun and everyone is familiar with

  H One that involves a lot of behind-the-scenes work

  J One that pays well

19 Who ensures that zoos do a good job caring for their animals?

  A A curator

  B A zookeeper

  C A charitable organization

  D A professional association

20 Where would a passage like this be most likely to appear?

  F In a popular magazine

  G On the front page of a newspaper

  H In a science book

  J On an advertisement for a city zoo

21 According to this passage —

  A zoos were developed only in the last century.

  B people have been fascinated by animals for thousands of years.

  C the first zoo in the world is in Philadelphia.

  D the best zoos were built during the Renaissance.

22 What is this passage mostly about?

  F Managing zoos

  G The history of zoos

  H Animals

  J Zoos

STOP

Example   Directions: Read the selection. Mark the answer you think is correct.

E1

The first attempts at human flight were made with a strange-looking device called an ornithopter. This odd aircraft uses the flapping movement of a pair of wings. You can buy a miniature ornithopter at a toy or hobby store, but no ornithopter large enough to carry a human has been invented yet.

Ornithopters were probably invented before planes because —

A   planes are expensive.

B   people were smaller.

C   people tried to imitate birds.

D   planes require fuel.

Ruler of the Jungle: Animated Repeat

Ruler of the Jungle, the newest Tiger adventure, is finally coming to theaters. Moviegoers have been eagerly awaiting the new animated movie for months. The first of the series, *Tiger Versus Trouble*, was a huge success, attracting millions of viewers. The sequel was also well received, with Terrance rescuing his friends, defeating the bad guys, and generally fighting evil and doing good. Audiences will not find the newest Tiger exploit so entertaining, however.

The scenery is still breathtakingly beautiful, and the music is rich and forceful, but the action is dull. The scenes seem to be a repeat of Terrance's earlier adventures. The action scenes seem so familiar, the viewer might wonder if the animators have tried to re-use some frames from the earlier movies.

Megamovie Company's latest production, like the previous two, is a technical marvel, blending photographic beauty with cartoon animation. *Ruler* will, no doubt, win awards for bringing together the real and the imaginary with such art. The music score is flawless; it will probably be a best-selling album.

The weakest part of the movie is the plot, which was the best part of the two earlier productions. Terrance again finds himself in trouble as he unwittingly stumbles into problems. He uses his intelligence, his strength, and his friends' assistance to overcome adversity and to help the good guys win. The problem with the story line is that it is too much like the other versions. Terrance does not have any really new adventures; they are all re-hashes of his old exploits. The only new addition is his love interest in Chloe, the lovely female tiger.

Small children will probably not notice the repetition, and students or adults who appreciate art and music will perhaps not care, but moviegoers who eagerly anticipated another good story will not find it in *Ruler of the Jungle*.

Natalie Nelson

1   This passage can best be described as—

    A   a review.

    B   an advertisement.

    C   an interview.

    D   a biography.

2   According to Natalie Nelson, what is the poorest part of the movie?

    F   The scenery and artwork

    G   The music

    H   The triumph of good over evil

    J   The lack of new adventures

3   Which word is used to describe the writer's opinion of the action in *Ruler of the Jungle*?

    A   Re-hash

    B   Exploits

    C   Animated

    D   Anticipated

4   Which character appears in *Ruler of the Jungle* but not in the two previous tiger movies?

    F   Terrance

    G   Terrance's friends

    H   The evil Dr. Snake

    J   Chloe

5   Which company produced *Ruler of the Jungle*?

    A   Technical Marvel

    B   Moviegoers

    C   Megamovie Company

    D   Tiger Adventure

6   *Ruler of the Jungle* is intended for —

    F   only young people.

    G   children, students, and adults.

    H   people who like adventure.

    J   animators.

7   From the passage, you can conclude that Terrance is —

    A   a person who rules the animals of the jungle fairly.

    B   a real tiger who survived as a cub in the jungle.

    C   an animated character who gets into different adventures.

    D   the producer of the three movies mentioned in the review.

GO

In this essay, a young man today tries to describe what it must have been like for his grandmother to come to America many years ago.

¶1 The year was 1914. In a few months, Archduke Francis Ferdinand, the heir to the Austrian throne, would be assassinated in Sarajevo. Woodrow Wilson was President of the United States, and a recent invention, the flying machine, was all the rage. Moving pictures were silent, and Edgar Rice Burroughs created a character for the ages, Tarzan of the Apes.

¶2 None of this, however, mattered to Mariana Potalivo, a fifteen-year old girl standing in a train station in the small Italian town. She and her brother, Nicholas, were taking the first step on a journey that would end almost halfway around the world in the most wonderful country she had ever heard of, America. Mariana was frightened of what lay ahead, but she was also excited. Besides, she had no choice. She had been promised in marriage to someone she had never even met, a young man from a nearby village who had already made the journey to America and who had found a most precious treasure, a job.

¶3 The small town of Compobasso was a very poor farming community in a poor country. Had she stayed in Compobasso, Mariana would have married a local boy, raised a family in the same house as his parents, and most likely never have traveled farther than Pescara, a city on the Adriatic coast. Her husband would have tried his best to scrabble out a living from the rocky soil, and her children would have done the same, as her family had done for over a thousand years.

¶4 The train ride across Italy to Naples was difficult. Although Francisco, her husband-to-be, had paid for Mariana's ticket on the ship, her parents had spent almost every cent they had on passage for her brother. Nicholas was only nine years old, but he was supposed to serve as her protector on the journey. The family had barely enough money left for two third-class train tickets to Naples. The two children sat on a hard bench for almost two days with dozens of other people, many of whom carried all their earthly possessions and who were making the same journey as Mariana and Nicholas. In addition, the third-class cars held farmers bringing their goods to market, from baskets of fruits and vegetables to chickens, goats, and pigs.

¶5 The children carried very few possessions themselves, some clothes, a photograph or two, and letters that would introduce them to people in America. Most of what they brought was food: cheese, dried fruit, bread, and sausage. They had no idea if anything would be available to eat on the train or the ship, and even if it was, they had only a few pennies to pay for it. Hour after hour they sat on the bench, swaying with the train, barely speaking, trying not to think of the family and friends they were leaving, perhaps forever. Both Mariana and Nicholas knew that going to America would open up a whole new life for them, but they were sad to be leaving the only life they had ever known.

¶6 When the train reached Naples early in the morning, they were tired and sore from the trip. They had no time to complain, however, because their ship would be leaving that afternoon. The children began the long walk from the railroad station to the dock, and even though they had never been to Naples before, had no difficulty finding the way. Hundreds of other people were doing exactly the same thing. All Mariana and Nicholas had to do was follow the crowd.

¶7 At the dock, Mariana and Nicholas stared at the ship, as did most of the other people in the crowd. It was the hugest thing they had ever seen, larger even than the church in Pescara. They slowly made their way up the gangplank and handed the steward their tickets. As they did, the realization of what was happening hit them. Once the ship left the dock, they would never set foot in Italy again, never sit in the town square on a warm summer evening and sing the old songs, never see their family again.

8 **In paragraph 4, what is the meaning of the word "passage"?**

F The trip to Naples

G A brief story

H The food the children carried

J The trip across the ocean

9 **Why does the writer begin with a description of world affairs in 1914?**

A World events would play an important part in the story.

B They help the reader understand the time period in which the story is set.

C They caused Mariana and her brother to leave their village.

D The children were interested in what was happening.

10 **How does the writer feel about his grandmother?**

F He admires her for undertaking such a difficult journey.

G He feels she gave up too much by leaving her village.

H He wishes she had been more aware of world affairs.

J He wishes she had stayed in her village in Italy.

11 **In paragraph 3, what is the Adriatic?**

A A small town

B A region of Italy

C A body of water

D A large city on the coast

12 **How did Mariana feel about marrying someone she had never met?**

F Unhappy and angry about having to leave her village

G Happy to have the opportunity to take a trip on a boat

H Disappointed because her brother had to go with her

J Willing to accept it because it was a tradition

13 **In paragraph 2, why is a job called a "precious treasure"?**

A The job paid very well.

B Not many people in the village had jobs.

C The job was in America.

D Jobs were easier to find in Italy than in America.

14 **Around 1914, it appears as if—**

F many other people were leaving Italy for America.

G only a few people were leaving Italy for America.

H the trip from Italy to America was easy and inexpensive.

J farming in Italy was a good way to earn a living.

GO

How did skiing change from necessity to sport?

Skiing today is a sport enjoyed by millions of Americans. More than a hundred years ago, however, people living in the West used skis for transportation, not recreation. The first Colorado skiers, for example, were miners looking for gold and silver in the 1860s. In the deep snows of winter, skis were the only way these miners could get around. Ministers, mail carriers, and even teachers were other early skiers in the Rocky Mountains.

Skiing was brought to America by settlers from Norway and other northern European countries. Their skis were long, wooden boards that looked very different from modern skis. And instead of two poles, early skiers used just one long pole to push themselves along. In addition to introducing Americans to skiing, European immigrants were responsible for founding many of America's ski resorts. The first Colorado ski resort opened in 1930, although other resorts in the East were started before that time.

In the early days of recreational skiing, people actually walked to the top of a mountain before they could ski down. Inventors soon solved that problem by creating various mechanical devices that could carry people up a mountain. This development helped skiing become more popular because it was so much easier to do. Another development that popularized skiing was a group of soldiers who trained for World War II in Colorado. Their heroics during the war influenced many people to take up the sport.

As more people learned to ski, resorts began to sponsor winter carnivals that included competitions. Steamboat Springs, Colorado, has had a festival every year since 1914, and almost every ski resort has a festival of one kind or another. The

Winter Olympics also focused a lot of attention on skiing, encouraging many Americans to take up the sport.

Vail, Colorado, has a ski museum that pays tribute to early American skiers. There you can learn about people who have been *inducted* into the Skiing Hall of Fame, like John Lewis Dyer, a minister who went around the mining camps in western Colorado on 11-foot handmade skis. You can also see the huge backpacks mail carriers used to deliver their letters and packages, see how equipment and skiing styles changed, and learn how skiing went from a necessity to a popular sport.

15 In the skiing museum, you would be most likely to find —

A pictures of the first Summer Olympics held in 1896.

B the latest ski fashions.

C ski boots that people wore in the 1940s.

D the names of the people who qualified for the next Olympics.

16 Mechanical devices to carry skiers up a mountain were invented soon after—

F the first downhill ski trails opened.

G skis were invented.

H skiing was used for transportation.

J the ski museum opened in Colorado.

17 After reading this passage, you should be able to —

A describe how Europeans invented skiing.

B explain how skiing became a sport.

C name the first ski resort in Colorado.

D name the first miner who used skis.

18 This story is *mainly* about —

F traveling by foot in the mountains of the American West.

G a sport brought to America by European immigrants.

H how modern technology changed a popular sport.

J how a sport developed from an activity that was a necessity.

19 In this passage, the word *inducted* means —

A made a member of.

B invited to speak at.

C visited often.

D helped to develop.

20 You can tell from this passage that —

F skis are longer today than they were in the past.

G gold and silver are found where there is a lot of snow.

H Steamboat Springs was the first ski resort in Colorado.

J people in Europe were skiing before Americans.

21 Skiing in America began in—

A the West.

B the East.

C areas where there was an Army base.

D the California mountains.

22 According to the article, skiing probably has become popular because of all these events except—

F Army skiers in World War II.

G the Winter Olympics.

H advertisements by ski manufacturers.

J the invention of the ski lift.

GO

ANSWER ROWS   **15** Ⓐ Ⓑ Ⓒ Ⓓ   **17** Ⓐ Ⓑ Ⓒ Ⓓ   **19** Ⓐ Ⓑ Ⓒ Ⓓ   **21** Ⓐ Ⓑ Ⓒ Ⓓ

16 Ⓕ Ⓖ Ⓗ Ⓙ   **18** Ⓕ Ⓖ Ⓗ Ⓙ   **20** Ⓕ Ⓖ Ⓗ Ⓙ   **22** Ⓕ Ⓖ Ⓗ Ⓙ

Grace Darling

The Darling family lived an isolated existence because the father was a lighthouse keeper on a rugged coastline in England. His job was to keep the beacon light burning so that ships would not pass too close to shore and be torn apart on the rocks. Mr. Darling worried that his lovely daughter, Grace, would miss out on too much of life if she stayed at the lighthouse, but he could not bear to be separated from his family. The loneliness he would have had to endure was not so bad as being kept apart from his loved ones. So the Darlings lived peacefully in the tall tower on the rocky shore, and Grace did her schoolwork under the direction of her mother. She fished, sailed, and explored with her father.

One night, after Mr. Darling had made sure the beacon was shining brightly across the ocean, a thunderstorm came up. Such storms were the only thing Grace did not like about living at the lighthouse. Sometimes it seemed that the wind would tear the building apart and scatter its boards and bricks across the sea. This night was worse than usual: the wind raged and howled, the lightning flashed, and the thunder rumbled and cracked. Grace and her parents were about to go down the circular stairs to their snug basement when she looked out the windows just as brilliant lightning lit up the entire sky.

"Father, look! There is a ship out there!" she cried.

"It will be all right, my dear," her father answered. "The light will warn them to steer clear of the rocks. Let's go below."

When the lightning flashed again, Mr. Darling watched in horror as the ship broke apart. With the next flash, the Darlings could see several survivors who had clung to the hull and were stuck on the rocks, holding on for dear life.

"Let's go out and rescue them," begged Grace.

"We can't go out in this storm," her father answered. "We will perish ourselves."

At last the storm seemed to lessen some, though it was still fierce; Mr. Darling finally relented. Grace insisted on going with him in their small boat. They rowed mightily against the raging waves and managed to reach the people. They fought their way back to the lighthouse. Grace and her father saved twelve lives that night. Mr. Darling gave Grace the credit because of her persistent pleading.

23 **Why did the lighthouse beacon not protect the ship from the rocks?**

　　A The sailors did not see it.

　　B It was not lit in time to help them.

　　C The storm blew the sailors into the rocks.

　　D The sailors ignored its warning.

24 **Which strategy would *best* help the reader understand this story?**

　　F Picturing what the Darlings' snug basement looked like

　　G Thinking about what fierce power storms can have

　　H Imagining what Grace and her father did in the boat

　　J Thinking about Grace's relationship with her father

25 **Why did Mr. Darling say his daughter was responsible for the rescue?**

　　A She insisted that they go out.

　　B She was too young to understand the danger.

　　C Rescue was not part of his job.

　　D She was a better rower than he was.

26 **In the second paragraph, Grace appears to be —**

　　F extremely brave.

　　G dutiful.

　　H observant.

　　J somewhat frightened.

27 **In the story, Grace showed that she was all of these *except* —**

　　A persistent.

　　B clever.

　　C sympathetic.

　　D brave.

28 **The *main* idea of this story is the importance of —**

　　F looking out the windows at the right time.

　　G being willing to help others when they are in need.

　　H taking care of family members first.

　　J knowing how to swim.

29 **The basement of the lighthouse is —**

　　A safer than the rest of it.

　　B large and beautiful.

　　C where the beacon is kept.

　　D damp and cold.

GO

For numbers 30 through 33, choose the best answer to the question.

An accident on the interstate this morning slowed rush hour traffic to a crawl. A truck loaded with bricks went out of control and overturned near Grand Avenue. This is the same section of road that caused the death of two motorists last month. It's time the state did something to improve the situation.

30 This passage would most likely be found in —

F a magazine article about bricks.

G an encyclopedia entry about trucks.

H a newspaper article about an accident.

J a review of an upcoming book.

31 Which of these sentences expresses a fact stated in the passage above?

A The state has done a poor job of taking care of the road.

B A truck loaded with bricks went out of control on the interstate.

C Traffic is usually heaviest during the morning rush hour.

D The section of interstate near Grand Avenue is the most dangerous.

32 Which of these statements makes use of a metaphor?

F The clouds blocked the sun, causing the temperature to drop.

G To Regina, the opposing team seemed much larger than her own.

H The crowd was a river, sweeping Gene through the stadium gates.

J The fish was so big we needed a second boat to haul it in.

33 Mary's heart sank when she heard her test score. It was good, but she wasn't sure it was high enough to earn her an A for the semester.

Which of these best explains the meaning of the phrase "Mary's heart sank"?

A She was very disappointed.

B She was very excited.

C Suddenly she couldn't breathe well.

D The test was easier than she had thought.

41

Name and Answer Sheet

To the Student:

These tests will give you a chance to put the tips you have learned to work.

A few last reminders...

- Be sure you understand all the directions before you begin each test. You may ask the teacher questions about the directions if you do not understand them.
- Work as quickly as you can during each test.
- When you change an answer, be sure to erase your first mark completely.

- You can guess at an answer or skip difficult items and go back to them later.
- Use the tips you have learned whenever you can.
- It is OK to be a little nervous. You may even do better.

Now that you have completed the lessons in this unit, you are on your way to scoring high!

STUDENT'S NAME — LAST — FIRST — MI

SCHOOL

TEACHER

FEMALE ○   MALE ○

BIRTH DATE

MONTH	DAY	YEAR

JAN FEB MAR APR MAY JUN JUL AUG SEP OCT NOV DEC

GRADE 7 8 9

PART 1　VOCABULARY

E1 Ⓐ Ⓑ Ⓒ Ⓓ　　6 Ⓕ Ⓖ Ⓗ Ⓙ　　13 Ⓐ Ⓑ Ⓒ Ⓓ　　20 Ⓕ Ⓖ Ⓗ Ⓙ　　27 Ⓐ Ⓑ Ⓒ Ⓓ　　31 Ⓐ Ⓑ Ⓒ Ⓓ
E2 Ⓕ Ⓖ Ⓗ Ⓙ　　7 Ⓐ Ⓑ Ⓒ Ⓓ　　14 Ⓕ Ⓖ Ⓗ Ⓙ　　21 Ⓐ Ⓑ Ⓒ Ⓓ　　28 Ⓕ Ⓖ Ⓗ Ⓙ　　32 Ⓕ Ⓖ Ⓗ Ⓙ
1 Ⓐ Ⓑ Ⓒ Ⓓ　　8 Ⓕ Ⓖ Ⓗ Ⓙ　　15 Ⓐ Ⓑ Ⓒ Ⓓ　　22 Ⓕ Ⓖ Ⓗ Ⓙ　　29 Ⓐ Ⓑ Ⓒ Ⓓ　　33 Ⓐ Ⓑ Ⓒ Ⓓ
2 Ⓕ Ⓖ Ⓗ Ⓙ　　9 Ⓐ Ⓑ Ⓒ Ⓓ　　16 Ⓕ Ⓖ Ⓗ Ⓙ　　23 Ⓐ Ⓑ Ⓒ Ⓓ　　30 Ⓕ Ⓖ Ⓗ Ⓙ　　34 Ⓕ Ⓖ Ⓗ Ⓙ
3 Ⓐ Ⓑ Ⓒ Ⓓ　　10 Ⓕ Ⓖ Ⓗ Ⓙ　　17 Ⓐ Ⓑ Ⓒ Ⓓ　　24 Ⓕ Ⓖ Ⓗ Ⓙ
4 Ⓕ Ⓖ Ⓗ Ⓙ　　11 Ⓐ Ⓑ Ⓒ Ⓓ　　18 Ⓕ Ⓖ Ⓗ Ⓙ　　25 Ⓐ Ⓑ Ⓒ Ⓓ
5 Ⓐ Ⓑ Ⓒ Ⓓ　　12 Ⓕ Ⓖ Ⓗ Ⓙ　　19 Ⓐ Ⓑ Ⓒ Ⓓ　　26 Ⓕ Ⓖ Ⓗ Ⓙ

PART 2　READING COMPREHENSION

E1 Ⓐ Ⓑ Ⓒ Ⓓ　　6 Ⓕ Ⓖ Ⓗ Ⓙ　　12 Ⓕ Ⓖ Ⓗ Ⓙ　　18 Ⓕ Ⓖ Ⓗ Ⓙ　　24 Ⓕ Ⓖ Ⓗ Ⓙ　　30 Ⓕ Ⓖ Ⓗ Ⓙ
1 Ⓐ Ⓑ Ⓒ Ⓓ　　7 Ⓐ Ⓑ Ⓒ Ⓓ　　13 Ⓐ Ⓑ Ⓒ Ⓓ　　19 Ⓐ Ⓑ Ⓒ Ⓓ　　25 Ⓐ Ⓑ Ⓒ Ⓓ　　31 Ⓐ Ⓑ Ⓒ Ⓓ
2 Ⓕ Ⓖ Ⓗ Ⓙ　　8 Ⓕ Ⓖ Ⓗ Ⓙ　　14 Ⓕ Ⓖ Ⓗ Ⓙ　　20 Ⓕ Ⓖ Ⓗ Ⓙ　　26 Ⓕ Ⓖ Ⓗ Ⓙ　　32 Ⓕ Ⓖ Ⓗ Ⓙ
3 Ⓐ Ⓑ Ⓒ Ⓓ　　9 Ⓐ Ⓑ Ⓒ Ⓓ　　15 Ⓐ Ⓑ Ⓒ Ⓓ　　21 Ⓐ Ⓑ Ⓒ Ⓓ　　27 Ⓐ Ⓑ Ⓒ Ⓓ　　33 Ⓐ Ⓑ Ⓒ Ⓓ
4 Ⓕ Ⓖ Ⓗ Ⓙ　　10 Ⓕ Ⓖ Ⓗ Ⓙ　　16 Ⓕ Ⓖ Ⓗ Ⓙ　　22 Ⓕ Ⓖ Ⓗ Ⓙ　　28 Ⓕ Ⓖ Ⓗ Ⓙ　　34 Ⓕ Ⓖ Ⓗ Ⓙ
5 Ⓐ Ⓑ Ⓒ Ⓓ　　11 Ⓐ Ⓑ Ⓒ Ⓓ　　17 Ⓐ Ⓑ Ⓒ Ⓓ　　23 Ⓐ Ⓑ Ⓒ Ⓓ　　29 Ⓐ Ⓑ Ⓒ Ⓓ　　35 Ⓐ Ⓑ Ⓒ Ⓓ

UNIT 3   TEST PRACTICE

Part 1   Vocabulary

Example

Directions: For E1, find the word that means the same or almost the same as the underlined word. For E2, read the question. Mark the answer you think is correct.

E1 sudden transition

A activity
B decision
C attack
D change

E2 Which of these probably comes from the Latin word *malus* meaning *pole*?

F malice
G must
H mast — a tall vertical pole to support a ships sails and rigging
J malt

For numbers 1-8, find the word or words that mean the same or almost the same as the underlined word.

1 nice attire

A foolish
B rapid
C dress
D painstaking

2 naturally expand

F attack
G grow
H weaken
J shrink

3 dwell nearby

A surround
B drink
C live
D chase

4 sensational story

F exaggerated
G dogmatic
H representative
J vigorous

5 Famine means about the same as —

A drastic shortage of food

A period of drought
B time of hunger
C great harvest
D rush to escape

6 Simmer means about the same as —

F cool
G boil quickly
H spill
J cook slowly

7 To capsize is to —

A turn over
B slow down
C soak
D speed up

8 If something is frivolous it is —

F cheap
G important
H unnecessary
J expensive

GO

9   A sudden <u>motion</u> scared the bird.

Motion means —

A movement
B sound
C wind
D storm

10   The <u>stray</u> calf wandered into a neighbor's yard.

Stray means —

F young
G happy
H frisky
J wandering

11   It started out as a <u>dismal</u> day.

If something is <u>dismal</u> it is —

A gloomy
B beautiful
C gorgeous
D busy

12   A <u>horde</u> of insects was in the garden.

Horde means —

F small group
G nest
H large group
J family

13   The <u>objective</u> was not very clear.

Objective means —

A agreement
B reason
C goal
D function

For numbers 14-19, find the word that means the opposite of the underlined word.

14   **candid answer**

F direct
G offensive
H hostile
J dishonest

15   **will <u>merge</u>**

A separate
B associate
C harden
D flow

16   **<u>entice</u> birds**

F attract
G ignore
H repel
J detract

17   **<u>persuade</u> his friends**

A convince
B discourage
C determine
D avoid

18   **a huge <u>windfall</u>**

F unexpected good luck
G expected result
H harsh criticism
J sad news

19   **<u>commotion</u> nearby**

A loud group
B working professionals
C school students
D quiet activity

GO

For numbers 20-23, choose the word that correctly completes <u>both</u> sentences.

20 She came up with a _____ solution.

The _____ I am reading has some interesting characters.

F great
G novel
H book
J surprising

21 This wall feels like it is _____ .

What was that loud _____ ?

A stable
B noise
C strong
D sound

22 A large navy _____ is located near my aunt's home.

We waited for our friends at the _____ of the mountain.

F yard
G base
H bottom
J dock

23 We may have to _____ to taking the train instead of driving.

The _____ had two swimming pools.

A change
B hotel
C resort
D agree

24 | A <u>scrap</u> of paper fell from his desk. |

In which sentence does the word <u>scrap</u> mean the same thing as in the sentence above?

F We'll have to <u>scrap</u> that idea.

G <u>Scrap</u> metal can be recycled and used again.

H Each <u>scrap</u> of cloth in the quilt held a memory for the family.

J The children began to <u>scrap</u> about who would sit in the front seat.

25 | The <u>express</u> train gets there at 9:00. |

In which sentence does the word <u>express</u> mean the same thing as in the sentence above?

A It is sometimes hard to <u>express</u> yourself.

B Leanna wanted to <u>express</u> the problem using an algebraic <u>formula</u>.

C We received an <u>express</u> order to finish this job today.

D <u>Express</u> shipping costs more but is worth the extra expense.

26 | The corn was <u>ground</u> with stone tools. |

In which sentence does the word <u>ground</u> mean the same thing as in the sentence above?

F The <u>ground</u> was soaked by heavy rain.

G <u>Ground</u> coffee loses its flavor faster than coffee beans.

H The leading candidate lost <u>ground</u> to her nearest competition.

J One of the wires in an electric circuit is called a <u>ground</u>.

GO

27 Which of these words probably comes from the Anglo-French word *taune* meaning *yellowish-brown*?

  A tawny
  B town
  C tread
  D tore

28 Which of these words probably comes from the Latin word *refugere* meaning *to flee*?

  F deploy
  G refugee
  H desolate
  J disintegrate

29 A _____ arose concerning the location of the new road.

Which of these words means an argument developed over the road?

  A conclusion
  B fellowship
  C mobilization
  D dispute

30 The mayor paid _____ visits to students in the school system.

Which of these words means the mayor visited occasionally?

  F constant
  G periodic
  H enjoyable
  J sudden

Read the paragraph. Find the word below the paragraph that fits best in each numbered blank.

The bicycle race had grown from a ___(31)___ to an international event. Thousands of riders now competed, not for money, but for the challenge. The race was only thirty miles long, not an ___(32)___ distance for a bicycle race, but it climbed four mountains that were each over ten thousand feet high. Only half of the racers who start the race ___(33)___ finish it. Those who do finish get only a shirt for all their efforts, and the ___(34)___ of being among just a handful of riders who are considered masters of the mountains.

31 **A** corrupt
      B lenient
      C friendly
      D local

32 **F** acceptable
      G inordinate
      H elaborate
      J ostentatious

33 **A** affirmatively
      B unusually
      C eventually
      D seemingly

34 **F** satisfaction
      G tribulation
      H insecurity
      J antagonist

STOP

Example

Directions: Read the selection. Mark the answer you think is correct.

E1

Don wasn't at all sure he wanted to ride the tram. It was the size of a large van and was suspended from three cables that stretched from the base of a mountain to the top, a distance of over two miles. It was supported by four towers, and at some points was over 400 feet above the ground. The tram had never had an accident, but Don was still frightened.

The tram in this story —

A   is two miles above the ground.

B   runs on four cables.

C   has a good safety record.

D   is the size of a large bus.

Here is a story about a very close call with lightning. Read the story and then do numbers 1 through 8 on page 49.

The storm started out like the others that summer, and there had been many of them. Clouds began to develop around three o'clock, they covered the sky completely by seven, and within half an hour, the rain came down in torrents. A little thunder and lightning added drama to the event, and then it all ended.

Jasmine stood by a window watching the rain fall when a bolt of lightning hit the house. At the same instant, a terrific crash of thunder shook everything. She jumped back from the window and clutched her chest. Jasmine had a hard time catching her breath and her heart was pounding like crazy.

"Are you all right, Jasmine?" Mr. Harrison rushed to her side with a worried look on his face.

"I'm okay, Dad. Boy, was that ever close. Did you see where it hit the house?"

"It looks like the lightning hit the television antenna. I wonder if anything was damaged. Run into the kitchen and try the phone. I'll turn the television on."

Jasmine ran into the kitchen and picked up the phone. There was a dial tone, so she hung up and ran back into the family room.

"The telephone still works, Dad. How's the television?"

"It works, but the color is way off. It will probably have to be repaired. Let's take a look outside. The storm is pretty much gone."

They walked around the house looking for signs of damage. There weren't any until they came to the television antenna. The antenna itself seemed to be fine, but the wire going into the house was blackened.

"Bingo, a direct hit. Let's check to see what happened inside."

The two of them walked back into the house and checked where the television antenna came in. Jasmine noticed that the antenna wire was beside the line to the second phone. She walked over to the table and picked it up. There was no dial tone.

"Dad, there's no dial tone on this phone. I'll bet the lightning jumped from the television wire to the telephone line and damaged the phone. What shall we do?"

"The phone company has a 24-hour service number. Why don't you give them a call and let them know what happened? If they want to set up a service appointment, I can stay home any morning this week. Your mother and brothers are going to be in for a surprise when they get home."

GO

1 This story suggests that the summer has been very —

    A stormy.

    B dry.

    C hot.

    D uneventful.

2 How did Jasmine discover that one of the phones didn't work?

    F Noticing the burned wire

    G Calling the number

    H Asking the service operator

    J Listening for a dial tone

3 What leads the reader to believe that Mr. Harrison has great confidence in Jasmine's ability?

    A He accepts Jasmine's judgment about how she feels.

    B He takes Jasmine outside to inspect the house.

    C He gives Jasmine the responsibility of calling the telephone service center.

    D He allows Jasmine to tell her mother and brothers what happened.

4 From this story, you can conclude that —

    F lightning is not likely to damage a television.

    G lightning can strike a house and not injure the people inside.

    H lightning occurs mainly at night or in the early evening.

    J televisions are built better than phones.

5 In this story, a hard rain is called —

    A a rush.

    B a bolt.

    C a drama.

    D a torrent.

6 Choose the sentence that tells what the passage is mostly about.

    F A girl and her father are in the house when lightning strikes it.

    G Two people repair the damage done by a lightning strike.

    H When lightning strikes a house, the two people in it panic.

    J A lightning strike damages most of the electrical circuits in a house.

7 When Jasmine's father says "Bingo," it indicates that —

    A the lightning strike caused damage but it wasn't serious.

    B the place where the lightning hit was on fire.

    C the phones in the house had escaped damage from the lightning.

    D he has found the place where the lightning struck.

8 In the beginning of the story, the author creates a sense of —

    F tragedy.

    G anger.

    H excitement.

    J relief.

GO

What would you have done?

For years, Jeremy had looked forward to being old enough to participate in the youth livestock show. His father had raised animals when he was a youngster, and Jeremy's two older sisters had won championships. Their trophies were all proudly displayed in the glass-front case in the dining room. Jeremy was sure that this year his would be added to the case. His prize pig, Cookie, "was a winner if he ever saw one," Jeremy's dad had said several times.

Jeremy had read dozens of articles furnished by his teacher. He had carefully mixed the food and vitamins that were recommended for a pig. His mother had driven him to a veterinarian's office twenty miles away to get a special vitamin supplement that would produce the healthy skin that Cookie needed to win. Jeremy walked Cookie for exercise and taught her to follow him around.

Mr. Henson and Jeremy had built a special pen, and Jeremy taught Cookie to push the automatic waterer with her nose to get a drink whenever she wanted it. Jeremy was convinced that pigs were the smartest animals.

Two weeks before the big show, Cookie was all ready. Everyone was proud and excited. Then something unexpected happened: Cookie got sick. The veterinarian came, but no one was sure exactly what caused the illness. She got better quickly, however, and was her old self after just a few days. Everyone in the family breathed a sigh of relief.

There was, however, one problem. Cookie had lost a lot of weight from the illness. She gained some of it back, but she was still several pounds too light and would be disqualified at the weigh-in. Jeremy was so disappointed that he was on the verge of tears because there was nothing he could do. Then his friend, Tim, said he had heard of some people who showed pigs and made them drink a lot of water so they would gain a few pounds. He said it would not hurt Cookie at all and it would be Jeremy's only chance to win.

Tim described what they would do to make Cookie drink the water. The more Tim talked, the worse Jeremy felt. He thought of how Cookie would feel after drinking all that water.

Jeremy looked at Tim and then looked at Cookie. He walked over to his pig, picked up her rope, and headed back to her pen. As he walked away, he heard Tim saying, "What's the matter, man? Don't you care anything about winning?"

"Not if it means hurting Cookie," Jeremy said. "She means too much to me. My little pig is more important than any old prize."

GO

9 **The message of this story is that —**

A   people should not get too attached to their pets.

B   some people are just not cut out to be winners.

C   it is sometimes difficult to make the right choice.

D   listening to friends is usually the right thing to do.

10 **There is enough information in this story to show that —**

F   Jeremy did his best to prepare Cookie for the competition.

G   Tim had a better attitude about winning than Jeremy.

H   Jeremy's teacher should have been paying closer attention to the boys.

J   Jeremy was too concerned about winning, like the rest of his family.

11 **Why did Cookie lose weight?**

A   Jeremy fed her the wrong things.

B   She didn't get enough water.

C   She ate too much.

D   She got sick.

12 **Jeremy did all of these things to make Cookie a champion pig except —**

F   read dozens of articles from his teacher.

G   run with her on a treadmill.

H   walk Cookie for exercise.

J   get a special vitamin for healthy skin.

13 **The veterinarian —**

A   suggested that Jeremy make Cookie drink more water.

B   did not know what caused Cookie's illness.

C   had treated Jeremy's sisters' show animals.

D   was also a judge in the youth livestock show.

14 **This story is organized according to —**

F   a main idea and supporting information.

G   an opening conclusion and examples.

H   an unusual set of comparisons.

J   a problem and a solution.

15 **To be disqualified is to be —**

A   forced to enter a competition.

B   invited to enter a competition.

C   eliminated from a competition.

D   disappointed by a competition.

16 **In this story, the reader learns that —**

F.   to be shown, pigs had to weigh a certain amount.

G   Jeremy's family had put a lot of pressure on him to win.

H   raising a show pig means you can't have other pets.

J   pigs are smarter than almost any other animal.

GO

A No-Guilt Treat

Most people like homemade ice cream in the summertime, but it can be loaded with fat and calories. Here is a treat that is easy to make and that may burn up more calories than it provides. The recipe is for orange sherbet, but you can vary the fruit flavor by using different kinds of soft drink.

You will need the following:
> Three large clean coffee cans
> Three small clean coffee cans
> Duct tape or other strong tape
> Crushed ice
> Ice cream salt or rock salt
> One can of sweetened condensed milk
> One can of crushed pineapple, with juice
> One two-liter bottle of orange soft drink
> Several friends or family members

Preparation method:
Mix the condensed milk, pineapple, and soft drink. Pour the mixture into a smaller coffee can, leaving a space of at least one-fourth of the volume for expansion as the sherbet freezes. Put the plastic lid on, and tape it firmly with duct tape. Be sure to go around the can several times to get a good seal so that no liquid from the outer can will get in. Set the small coffee can in the center of a large can. Fill the space between the cans with crushed ice and a generous amount of rock salt. The rock salt will help the ice freeze the sherbet mix more quickly. Shake the can to settle the ice and add more ice and salt. The ice and salt mix should be packed firmly. Put on the plastic lid and carefully tape it in place. Be sure the tape makes several continuous loops across the top and bottom of each can. Repeat the process with the remainder of the mixture and the other two cans.

The people who expect to enjoy the sherbet should toss, kick, throw, and roll the cans around for 30 to 45 minutes. The more activity there is, the better the sherbet will be. After a few minutes of agitation, frost will begin to form on the outside can. When this happens, you know that the freezing is taking place.

When you think the sherbet has had time to freeze, open the outer can, pour out the water, add more ice and salt, and wait as long as you can stand it. This step will ripen and firm the sherbet. Then get the bowls and spoons and enjoy your no-guilt treat!

GO

17 Agitating the can consists of all of the following *except* —

A rolling the can.

B tossing the can.

C setting the can down.

D kicking the can.

18 You could also make this recipe with —

F an electric ice cream freezer.

G one large plastic bucket and ice.

H an ice cube tray and freezer.

J two paper bags of different size.

19 If you wanted to make ice cream instead of sherbet, which part of the instructions would you have to change?

A Use ordinary table salt and ice cubes instead of crushed ice and rock salt.

B Use strawberry soda instead of orange.

C Nothing needs to be changed.

D Use an ice cream recipe or mix instead of the one given.

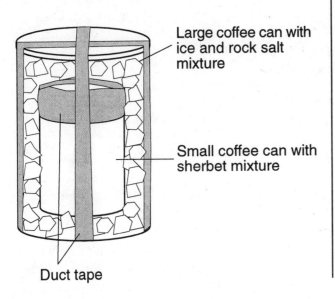

Large coffee can with ice and rock salt mixture

Small coffee can with sherbet mixture

Duct tape

20 This recipe is good for a family picnic because —

F it requires group participation and is good to eat.

G leftovers can be stored in the freezer or an ice chest.

H it does not have many ingredients.

J several people can be served.

21 The phrase "as long as you can stand it" was put in the recipe to suggest that —

A the longer the sherbet ripens, the better it will taste.

B the cold sherbet will make everyone around it cold.

C people will have a hard time waiting for the sherbet to be ready.

D it will take a long time for the sherbet to ripen.

22 The rock salt —

F flavors the sherbet.

G keeps the cans from making noise.

H prevents spoilage.

J makes the ice work faster.

23 Another good name for this recipe would be —

A "Almost Ice Cream."

B "Can-can Sherbet."

C "An Interesting Dessert."

D "Good and Cold."

Read the passage and questions on the next page. Choose the answer that is better than the others.

If you ever wanted to write a book about little-known Americans who have made significant contributions to the country, your subjects would include people like Grace Hopper, a computer scientist, Charles Drew, the inventor of the blood bank, or Luis Alvarez, one of the creators of the guidance system that allows planes to land in difficult weather. Your book would also include an obscure character who, in his time, was larger than life, John Charles Frémont.

Born in Savannah, Georgia, in 1813, Frémont was known as "the Pathfinder" because of his explorations of the American West. He was appointed to the Army Topographic Corps and joined the Nicollet expedition to map the region between the upper Mississippi and Missouri Rivers. In 1842, he was given his own expedition to survey the Oregon Trail. His success led to a second expedition, the exploration of much of the West that was still uncharted territory. His hardships and deprivations made news around the country, and for a time, he was perhaps the most famous person in America.

To understand how difficult exploration was for Frémont and his men, consider this: there was not a single road through the Rocky or Sierra Mountains. Frémont's expedition was often traveling in winter at elevations above 10,000 feet with limited supplies of food and clothing. They had no accurate maps, yet they successfully traversed an area that is about one-third the size of the forty-eight contiguous states.

When he returned East, much of the information gathered by Frémont was considered to be ridiculous, yet it was true. He verified the existence of the Salt Lake in Utah and described a Great Basin between the Rockies and the Sierra mountains. He found the best pass through the mountains, and proved false the idea that there was a great river that flowed due west from the Rockies to the Pacific Ocean.

At the conclusion of his second expedition, Frémont moved to California, a land he had come to love on his journey. He was one of the moving forces behind the attempt to gain independence for California from Spain, which finally occurred in 1848. Frémont contributed in many ways to the development of California, and was one of its first senators to the U.S. Congress. When gold was discovered in California, Frémont was among the many who became rich overnight. As history has proven, this was the high point of his life.

Because of his popularity among the general public and his strong stand against slavery, Frémont was chosen to run for President by the newly formed Republican party. He was defeated by James Buchanan and returned to California. When the Civil War broke out, he fought for the Union, holding the rank of major general. He was not an effective general, which, combined with his strong opinions, caused him to leave the army.

After the war, Frémont's fortunes continued to slide. He mismanaged his land holdings and made poor investments, losing most of his fortune. He was appointed as governor of the Arizona Territory from 1878 to 1883, after which he again returned to California. He died in 1890 while on a visit to New York City.

Throughout his life, John Charles Frémont was a controversial figure. He constantly sought the support of political figures for personal advancement and married the daughter of the powerful senator, Thomas Hart Benton. During his expeditions, he often ignored direct orders, yet seemingly followed "secret" orders given from above. His men were extremely loyal to him, even though he put them in constant danger and many died. He was an instigator of the California rebellion that brought the region under U.S. control, but seemed to be doing it for personal gain. In the army, Frémont was found guilty of disobedience and unacceptable conduct, but he received a Presidential pardon. Despite these controversies, no one can dispute the fact that Frémont's courage and determination opened up the West and hastened America's rise to greatness.

24 **What was the purpose of the Army Topographic Corps?**

   F To seek independence for California

   G To build roads through the Rockies

   H To explore and make maps

   J To build towns in the West

25 **In the first paragraph, what does the word "obscure" mean?**

   A Little-known

   B Famous

   C Successful

   D Highly regarded

26 **What does it mean to say Frémont was a "moving force" behind the attempt to gain independence for California?**

   F He moved to California because it would soon be independent.

   G He was one of the people who wanted independence, but did not want to fight for it.

   H He was one of the people who was not sure about independence.

   J He was one of the people who worked hard for independence.

27 **When Frémont first arrived in California —**

   A it was a Spanish possession.

   B it had recently gained independence.

   C it was an American state.

   D gold had just been discovered.

28 **What is this passage mainly about?**

   F The exploration of the American West

   G What it takes to run for President

   H A little-known American hero

   J How politics can cause the fall of a hero

29 **Why were Frémont's men loyal even though he put them in danger?**

   A He respected them and they knew the importance of their job.

   B They feared him and the President.

   C They were interested in getting rich.

   D They didn't mind traveling through the mountains in the winter.

30 **Why would the President have granted Frémont a pardon?**

   F Frémont was working under secret orders from another country.

   G There was little evidence to prove Frémont was a troublemaker.

   H Frémont promised to help California become independent.

   J Despite his problems, Frémont had accomplished a great deal.

31 **Why does the author believe that the discovery of gold in California was the high point of Frémont's life?**

   A He had more money then than he ever would again.

   B From that point onward, most of what he tried ended in failure.

   C Being rich is more important than running for President.

   D He accomplished nothing before and nothing afterward.

GO >

For numbers 32 and 33, choose the best answer to the question.

32   The detective walked into the dining room and noticed a strange odor. It was not unpleasant, nor was it strong. She couldn't identify the odor, but she knew she had smelled it before.

This passage was probably taken from —

F   a mystery.

G   a comedy.

H   a science story.

J   an historical novel.

33   The top of the cliff was twenty yards away. Woodie looked over the face of the cliff and spotted a dozen handholds. He reached deep within himself, grasped the nearest handhold, and made his way toward the top.

Which of these best explains the meaning of the phrase "reached deep within himself"?

A   Fought off fear

B   Considered how he would climb up

C   Looked for a way down

D   Relied on his last reserves of energy

Read this passage. Then do numbers 34 and 35.

The cliffs near Centralia are actually made of volcanic rock that is about 2 million years old. The view from the top is spectacular, and the cave near the crest is the favorite spot for tourists. The walk up is long and tiring but worth the effort.

34   **This passage would most likely be found in —**

F   a report on volcanoes.

G   a travel brochure.

H   an encyclopedia entry about cliffs.

J   a newspaper article about walking.

35   **Which of these is a fact expressed in the passage?**

A   The walk up is long and tiring but worth the effort.

B   The cave is the favorite spot for tourists.

C   The cliffs are made of volcanic rock about 2 million years old.

D   The view from the top is spectacular.

Table of Contents
Language

Lesson 1   Punctuation

Examples   **Directions:** Mark the space for the punctuation mark that is needed in the sentence. Mark the space for "None" if no more punctuation marks are needed.

A   Pete how did you finish your dinner so quickly?

    A ,   **B** ;   **C** :   **D** None

B   The judges chose three finalists: Tonya, Albert, and Leticia.

    F ?   **G** "   **H** .   **J** None

Tips

Read the sentence. First check the end punctuation, then check for missing punctuation inside the sentence.

If you are not sure which answer choice is correct, look at the answer choices. Ask yourself: "Are any of these punctuation marks needed in the sentence?"

Practice

1   "Grab that rope" yelled the deck hand.

    A .   **B** !   **C** ,   **D** None

2   This house, I should add, is selling for less than it cost when it was built.

    F :   **G** "   **H** ,   **J** None

3   The officer asked, "Is there some way I can help?

    A "   **B** ,   **C** .   **D** None

4   The contents of the package pleased everyone homemade cookies, fruit, and brownies.

    F ,   **G** ;   **H** :   **J** None

5   No the telephone is not for you.

    A ;   **B** ,   **C** :   **D** None

6   "Let's get started before the crowd arrives," suggested Bandar

    F .   **G** ,   **H** !   **J** None

GO ▷

For numbers 7-13, read each answer. Fill in the space for the choice that has a punctuation error. If there is no mistake, fill in the fourth answer space.

7 **A** Several things had been knocked
   B to the floor by the quake a pot,
   C a bag of groceries, and a chair.
   D *(No mistakes)*

8 **F** Trees, shrubs, and, wildflowers
   G grew on the hillside because
   H of the water provided by the spring.
   J *(No mistakes)*

9 **A** Although the house is
   B on a busy street, it is quiet because
   C of a well-placed wall.
   D *(No mistakes)*

10 **F**
    G   Central High School
    H   Aldan, IL 62988
    J   March 23 1995,
       (No mistakes)

11 **A** Randford University
    B Median, IL 60513
    C Dear Dean Fortney
    D *(No mistakes)*

12 **F** Please send me a copy of your catalog.
    G of summer courses. I am a high school
    H student and would like to take a course.
    J *(No mistakes)*

13 **A** I look forward to receiving the catalog.
    B   Sincerely,
    C   *Wotan Pawlski*
    D *(No mistakes)*

For numbers 14-17, read each sentence with a blank. Choose the word or words that fit best in the blank and show the correct punctuation.

14 Remember to bring your _____ you will not be admitted to the reception.

   F invitation; or
   G invitation, or
   H invitation or,
   J invitation or

15 The _____ face was covered with dust and sweat.

   A riders
   B rider's
   C riders'
   D riders's

16 After you type this _____ I will make the copies we need for the meeting.

   F report Jacob
   G report, Jacob:
   H report, Jacob,
   J report, Jacob

17 _____ wondered Adrian, looking at the ruins in the valley.

   A "Why do you think they left?"
   B "Why do you think they left."
   C "Why do you think they left,"
   D "Why do you think they left"

STOP

ANSWER ROWS   7 Ⓐ Ⓑ Ⓒ Ⓓ   10 Ⓕ Ⓖ Ⓗ Ⓙ   13 Ⓐ Ⓑ Ⓒ Ⓓ   16 Ⓕ Ⓖ Ⓗ Ⓙ
              8 Ⓕ Ⓖ Ⓗ Ⓙ   11 Ⓐ Ⓑ Ⓒ Ⓓ   14 Ⓕ Ⓖ Ⓗ Ⓙ   17 Ⓐ Ⓑ Ⓒ Ⓓ
              9 Ⓐ Ⓑ Ⓒ Ⓓ   12 Ⓕ Ⓖ Ⓗ Ⓙ   15 Ⓐ Ⓑ Ⓒ Ⓓ

59

Examples   **Directions:** Mark the space for the answer that shows correct punctuation and capitalization. Mark the space for "Correct as it is" if the underlined part is correct.

A A All of us wi'll have to help.

B Dont' carry more boxes than you can handle easily.

C This shouldn't be too heavy for you.

D We have'nt finished, but we can stop now for a break.

B If <u>necessary, we</u> can mail it to you.

F necessary. We

G necessary we,

H necessary: we

J Correct as it is

Remember, you are looking for the answer that shows correct capitalization and punctuation.

Skip difficult items and come back to them later.

Practice

1 A Our house was built in 1990; theirs was built in 1994.

B Joe walked with Linda; As far as the playground.

C Most of the trees in this neighborhood, were planted between 1970 and 1980.

D One of the nicest things about living here is: the park.

2 F On this trip my Father visited Texas.

G One of the hardest parts of a vacation, is getting to the Airport on time.

H While waiting in the airport, Ken was able to call his parents.

J After the plane took off, another plane, took its place at the Gate.

3 A "Do you know where we can buy some poster board." wondered George.

B "A craft store is on Palmer street," suggested Sally.

C Lou Ella commented "we can't take the bus there."

D "Is that the only craft store in town?" asked Carl.

4 "Your room is on the fifth floor," said the <u>clerk, "And</u> the pool is on the roof."

F clerk "and

G clerk, "and

H clerk; "and

J Correct as it is

5 The <u>stores</u> construction was delayed because of a trucking strike.

A stores'

B stores's

C store's

D Correct as it is

6 The <u>ball and</u> your shoes are in the closet.

F ball, and

G ball and,

H ball, and,

J Correct as it is

GO

One of the newest ways of keeping a house warm is radiant

(7) heating; coils of plastic tubing are built into the floor or slab of the

(8) house. When it becomes necessary to heat the house hot water is

forced through the tubing. The floor becomes warm, and because

(9) heat rises, so does the air in the rest of the house. It is an efficient

(10) heating system. That is becoming more and more popular.

7
A heating, coils
B heating. Coils
C heating: Coils
D Correct as it is

8
F house, hot
G house. Hot
H House. Hot
J Correct as it is

9
A the house, it
B the House, it
C the house; it
D Correct as it is

10
F system, that
G system; that
H system that
J Correct as it is

January 18, 1995

(11) Kimmon Travel Co,
1314 Branford Avenue
Solex, ID 83109

(12) Dear Mrs. Willis:

(13) Thank you for sending us *A Guide to the Idaho mountains*. It

(14) arrived yesterday but our tickets did not. Could you please give us
a call and let us know when to expect them?

Sincerely yours,

Jane Gibbons

11
A Kimmon Travel Co
B Kimmon Travel Co.
C Kimmon travel co.
D Correct as it is

12
F Dear Mrs. Willis,
G Dear Mrs Willis:
H Dear Mrs. Willis;
J Correct as it is

13
A *Idaho Mountains*.
B *idaho mountains*.
C *Idaho Mountains*?
D Correct as it is

14
F yesterday; but
G yesterday; but,
H yesterday, but
J Correct as it is

GO ▷

ANSWER ROWS   7 (A)(B)(C)(D)   9 (A)(B)(C)(D)   11 (A)(B)(C)(D)   13 (A)(B)(C)(D)
8 (F)(G)(H)(J)   10 (F)(G)(H)(J)   12 (F)(G)(H)(J)   14 (F)(G)(H)(J)

61

For numbers 15 and 16, read the sentence with a blank. Mark the space beside the answer choice that fits best in the blank and has correct capitalization and punctuation.

15 The dog is _____ went for a long hike with us.

    A sleeping, She
    B sleeping; she
    C sleeping: She
    D sleeping she

16 The other night my family had dinner at _____

    F an Indian restaurant.
    G an indian restaurant.
    H an Indian Restaurant.
    J an Indian, restaurant.

Lydia wrote this report about the history of technology. Read the report and use it to do numbers 17-20.

```
     When they talk about technological advances,
        (1)
most people think about Telephones and Satellites.

They forget that every civilization had its own
(2)
kind of advances. Ancient humans, for example,
                        (3)
discovered fire, the wheel, and agriculture. These
                                          (4)
discoveries don't sound very hi-tech: but they laid

the foundation for the advanced civilizations of

Africa, Europe, and the americas
```

17 In sentence 1, **Telephones and Satellites** is best written —

    A telephone's and satellite's
    B telephones' and satellites'
    C telephones and satellites
    D As it is

18 In sentence 3, **humans, for example,** is best written —

    F humans for example
    G humans. For example
    H humans for example,
    J As it is

19 In sentence 4, **hi-tech: but** is best written —

    A hi-tech, but
    B hi-tech. But
    C hi-tech; But
    D As it is

20 In sentence 4, **the americas** is best written —

    F the America's.
    G the Americas.
    H the Americas'.
    J As it is

STOP

Example   Directions: Fill in the answer choice for the punctuation mark that is needed in the sentence. If no punctuation is needed you should fill in the answer choice for "None".

E1

"We're number one!" shouted the fans as the clock ran out.

A ,   B ;   C :   D None

---

1 You will have your choice of several trips the museum, the space center, or the university.

A :   B ;   C ,   D None

2 Ned your report about agriculture was the best you have ever written.

F !   G ;   H ,   J None

3 The news weather, and sports can be heard on the radio each hour.

A :   B ,   C ;   D None

4 The interstate is clogged with traffic; the surface roads are almost empty.

F ;   G ,   H :   J None

For numbers 5-7, read each answer. Fill in the space for the choice that has a punctuation error. If there is no mistake, fill in the fourth answer space.

5 A "I didn't do it," argued Nancy.
   B "I was at the library from
   C noon until five o'clock."
   D *(No mistakes)*

6 F My brother writes a column;
   G for our local newspaper.
   H It's about sports in schools.
   J *(No mistakes)*

7 A It was becoming clear that
   B wed' taken the wrong trail
   C and were heading away from the lake.
   D *(No mistakes)*

For numbers 8 and 9, read each sentence with a blank. Choose the word or words that fit best in the blank and show the correct punctuation.

8 Kevin, _____ found the puppy wandering around the school.

   F not Sharon,
   G not Sharon
   H not Sharon:
   J not, Sharon

9 The kitchen is too _____ let's eat on the back porch.

   A hot
   B hot,
   C hot:
   D hot;

GO

For numbers 10-13, read each group of words. Find the sentence that is written correctly and shows the correct capitalization and punctuation.

10 **F** "It's so good to see you," said Donna to her old friend Kent.

   G "This is my first class reunion, commented Lena."

   H Abbie suggested "we should try to get together more often."

   J Amos, said, "I can't believe so many people showed up"

11 **A** Clocks, and watches are on sale this weekend at sanborns department store.

   B Harold's designs, is one of the newest stores in the mall.

   C Stamps, boxes, and wrapping paper are available at the Joyce's Gift Shop.

   D The school store sells pens paper and other school supplies.

12 **F** We had a funny experience in a small town, in new York.

   G Matlock, the town next to ours, has a music festival each summer.

   H Many people are discovering, the attractions in their own States.

   J Large cities like Chicago and san Francisco, have many summer events.

13 **A** Nellie, tried to fix the leaky faucet in the bathroom.

   B If you see, Lloyd, let him know I am looking for him.

   C It's your turn Brandon

   D Pancho, did you call me?

For numbers 14-17, read the sentence with a blank. Mark the space beside the answer choice that fits best in the blank and has correct capitalization and punctuation.

14 The _____ because it is near the ocean, has lots of rain.

   F northwest
   G northwest,
   H Northwest;
   J Northwest,

15 The Pet Emporium is at _____ , right beside the gas station.

   A 23 Randolph St.
   B 23 Randolph st.
   C 23 randolph st.
   D 23 randolph st

16 The Grand Canyon, which is in Arizona, is one of our most popular _____ .

   F National Parks
   G National parks
   H national parks
   J national Parks

17 _____ suggested Susanna.

   A "Let's walk to the park,"
   B "Lets walk to the park,"
   C "let's walk to the park,"
   D "Let's walk to the Park,"

GO

For numbers 18-21, look at the underlined part of each sentence. Find the answer choice that shows the correct capitalization and punctuation for the underlined part.

18 Linda <u>announced "The</u> winner of the contest is Millie Anderson."

    F announced, "the

    G announced, "The

    H announced ",The

    J Correct as it is

19 If you want to know my <u>opinion, I</u> think she did the right thing.

    A opinion I

    B opinion: I

    C opinion? I

    D Correct as it is

20 The gym closes at noon on <u>Saturday, the</u> library is open until six o'clock.

    F saturday. The

    G Saturday: the

    H Saturday; the

    J Correct as it is

21 The computer is <u>new but</u> the printer is three years old.

    A new, but

    B new. But

    C new; but

    D Correct as it is

For numbers 22-25, read the passage. Find the answer choice that shows the correct capitalization and punctuation for the underlined part.

(22)   "Are you sure this is the right <u>color?" asked</u> Mrs. Georgio. She

(23)   looked at the walls the <u>painter's had</u> already completed and then at the fabric sample. The client for whom she was working was

(24)   very <u>picky and</u> Mrs. Georgio did not want to offend him. Her design business was successful because Mrs. Georgio paid close

(25)   attention to details. If the paint was not <u>correct, doctor</u> Martin would certainly notice.

22 **F** color," asked
    G color," Asked
    H color asked,"
    J Correct as it is

23 **A** painters had
    B painters' had
    C painters, had
    D Correct as it is

24 **F** picky; and
    G picky. And
    H picky, and
    J Correct as it is

25 **A** correct Doctor
    B correct, Doctor
    C correct. Doctor
    D Correct as it is

GO

This is more of Lydia's report about technology. Read the report and use it to do numbers 26-29.

Technology has always built upon <u>itself, fire,</u>
(1)
for example, was discovered accidentally, probably

as the result of a lightning-started brush fire.

Once humans learned to use fire and make it
(2)
themselves, they were able to create metals from

ore. With metals such as bronze and iron, humans
(3)
could make better <u>tools: utensils,</u> and weapons.

Fire technology, in other words, led to metal
(4)
technology.

Another thing that technology does is improve
(5)
life. Fire creates light, so humans could stay up
(6)
later at night. They could also stay warmer in cold
(7)
weather and even move into areas that were too cold

before. Primitive <u>humans ability</u> to live in
(8)
<u>northern Europe</u> and Asia was the result of the

discovery of fire.

26 In sentence 1, <u>itself, fire,</u> is best written —

  F itself: fire,
  G itself fire
  H itself. Fire,
  J As it is

27 In sentence 3, <u>tools: utensils,</u> is best written —

  A tools utensils
  B tools utensils,
  C tools, utensils,
  D As it is

28 In sentence 8, <u>humans ability</u> is best written —

  F human's ability
  G humans' ability
  H humans, ability
  J As it is

29 In sentence 8, <u>northern Europe</u> is best written —

  A northern Europe,
  B Northern Europe
  C Northern Europe,
  D As it is

66

STOP

Examples   **Directions:** Read the directions for each section. Fill in the circle for the answer you think is correct.

Choose the word that best completes the sentence.	**Choose the answer that is a complete and correctly written sentence.**
A The coat _____ you bought last year still looks brand new.	**B** **F** The maps you gave Ben and I will help us plan our trip.
(A) that	**G** Me and him are taking the train today.
B this	**H** Karen saw Matt and I, but we didn't see her.
C who	**J** She and I are going to the movies tomorrow afternoon.
D when	

If you are not sure which answer choice is correct, eliminate answers you know are wrong and then take your best guess.

It might help to say each answer choice to yourself. If an item has a blank, try each answer choice in the blank and say the completed sentence to yourself.

Practice

For numbers 1-3, choose the word or phrase that best completes the sentence.

1 Richard let _____ into the house.

A myself

B his

(C) himself

D we

2 The farmer _____ the crops already.

F will plant

G has planted

H plants

J have planted

3 This game is _____ than the other one.

(A) more challenging

B most challenging

C challenging

D challenged

For numbers 4-6, choose the answer that is a complete and correctly written sentence.

4 **F** The rivers in our state is cleaner because of a new law.

G Planting trees or shrubs help to hold the soil along rivers.

H The birds beside the road don't seems to mind the traffic.

J The stars seem especially bright tonight.

5 **A** Haven't you got no pencil or paper?

B She couldn't find your phone number.

C I didn't have no idea where you lived.

D Lee hadn't never been to your house.

6 **F** Kim is the one who found the keys.

G Who's hat is under the kitchen table?

H The pen what you are looking for is here.

J A shopper which was here yesterday forgot her umbrella.

GO

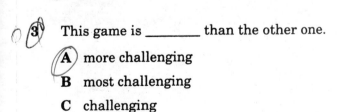

ANSWER ROWS   **A** Ⓐ Ⓑ Ⓒ Ⓓ   **1** Ⓐ Ⓑ Ⓒ Ⓓ   **3** Ⓐ Ⓑ Ⓒ Ⓓ   **5** Ⓐ Ⓑ Ⓒ Ⓓ

B Ⓕ Ⓖ Ⓗ Ⓙ   **2** Ⓕ Ⓖ Ⓗ Ⓙ   **4** Ⓕ Ⓖ Ⓗ Ⓙ   **6** Ⓕ Ⓖ Ⓗ Ⓙ

For numbers 7-12, read each answer choice. Fill in the space for the choice that has a usage error. If there is no mistake, fill in the fourth answer space.

7 **A** The most exciting thing that
    B happened to us was a flat tire. A
    C movie star stopped to help us!
    D *(No mistakes)*

8 **F** The job we did was acceptable,
    G but we coulda done even better
    H if we had been given more time.
    J *(No mistakes)*

9 **A** The walkathon was great, but
    B by the time we were finished,
    C we were really wore out.
    D *(No mistakes)*

10 **F** The fishes you saw were salmon.
    G They return from the ocean each
    H year and spawn in this creek.
    J *(No mistakes)*

11 **A** I don't know about the rest of
    B you, but I am certain that
    C Denine and me will be ready.
    D *(No mistakes)*

12 **F** The most likely person to be
    G chosen is Ishmael. He has been training
    H the longest and were in great shape.
    J *(No mistakes)*

For numbers 13 and 14, choose the best way to write the underlined part of each sentence. If the underlined part is correct, fill in the fourth answer space.

13 <u>However</u> it is cold, the sun is shining and it feels warmer than it really is.

    A Yet
    B Although
    C Despite
    D *(No change)*

14 The traffic <u>was heavy</u> next week because a convention will be in town.

    F will be heavy
    G were heavy
    H is heavy
    J *(No change)*

For numbers 15 and 16, choose the answer that is a complete and correctly written sentence.

15 **A** With his tail wagging, Bill threw the stick to the eager dog.
    B While taking a test, a bird flew into our classroom and out again.
    C Before buying the bicycle, the clerk told me it was on sale.
    D Just before she left, Adona reminded us to close the windows.

16 **F** The newest store in the mall, which is a nature shop.
    G You can borrow this book, remembering to return it in a week.
    H On our way here, we saw a flock of geese land in a field.
    J Pull the shades down, with the sun coming in through the window.

GO

Here is more of the report Lydia wrote about technology. Read the report and use it to do numbers 17-20.

Technology often has its beginning in nature.
       (1)
Fire, which was mentioned earlier, is one example.
    (2)
Another is the basket. Primitive humans probably
     (3)   (4)
using the nests of large birds as the first

baskets. They soon learned to weave their own
              (5)
baskets by imitating the structure of a nest.

Eventually, as finer materials such as grasses were
(6)
used, humans learned to weave cloth.

   Some of the technologies discovered by primitive
        (7)
humans remain a mystery today. Scientists still
                                 (8)
don't know, for example, that the pyramids were

built. Huge stones weighing many tons had to be
         (9)
lifted over a hundred feet. This would be a
                                       (10)
difficult feat even today, but Egyptians they were

able to do it more than 4,000 years ago.

17 In sentence 2, earlier is best written —

A early
B earliest
C more early
D As it is

18 In sentence 4, using the nests is best written —

F use the nests
G used the nests
H uses the nests
J As it is

19 In sentence 8, that the pyramids is best written —

A which the pyramids
B like the pyramids
C how the pyramids
D As it is

20 In sentence 10, Egyptians they were is best written —

F Egyptians were
G Egyptians was
H Egyptians they was
J As it is

Examples   **Directions:** Read the directions for each section. Fill in the circle
for the answer you think is correct.

Choose the simple subject of the sentence.	Mark the answer choice that best combines the underlined sentences.
A The bank gave a radio to new customers.	
A B C D	C It is snowing.
Choose the simple predicate (verb) of the sentence.	The snow is not falling hard.
B A wide river blocked the traveler's progress.	A It is snowing, and not hard.
F G H J	B Although not hard, it is snowing.
	C It is not snowing, but hard.
	D It is snowing, but not hard.

Stay with your first answer choice. You should change an answer
only if you are sure the one you chose is wrong.

Remember, the subject comes before the verb in most sentences.

Practice

For numbers 1-3, find the underlined part that is the simple subject of the sentence.

1   The officer stopped the truck for a safety inspection.
      A   B   C   D

2   The two regional winners are from Illinois and Wisconsin.
     F   G   H   J

3   After lunch, the students remained in the cafeteria for a movie about nutrition.
      A   B   C   D

For numbers 4-6, find the underlined part that is the simple predicate (verb) of the sentence.

4   A deep puddle formed under the bridge.
     F   G   H   J

5   Visitors enter the museum through a pair of huge doors.
      A   B   C   D

6   With the saddle off, the horse raced around the field faster than before.
     F   G   H J

GO

For numbers 7-9, choose the answer that best combines the underlined sentences.

7 Tickets for this concert are free.

You must order tickets ahead of time.

   A You must order tickets ahead of time, and tickets for this concert are free.

   B Tickets for this concert are free, despite you must order them ahead of time.

   C Tickets for this concert are free; you must, however, order them ahead of time.

   D You must order tickets ahead of time, or tickets for this concert are free.

8 The radio station is having a contest for student announcers.

We visited the radio station last week.

   F The radio station, which we visited last week, is having a contest for student announcers.

   G Because we visited the radio station last week, it is having a contest for student announcers.

   H The radio station, that we visited last week, and is having a contest for student announcers.

   J A contest for student announcers, which is by the radio station that we visited last week.

9 A deer stepped into the road.

The car swerved to avoid it.

The car narrowly missed the deer.

   A A deer stepped into the road, and a car swerved to avoid it, and the car narrowly missed the deer.

   B Swerving to avoid it, the deer stepped into the road and was narrowly missed by the car.

   C The car, which narrowly missed the deer, had swerved to avoid it, as the deer stepped into the road.

   D The car swerved to avoid a deer that stepped into the road, narrowly missing it.

For numbers 10 and 11, choose the best way of expressing the idea.

10 **F** Having just built a house, the volunteers stepped back, filled with pride, and admired it.
     G Filled with pride, the volunteers stepped back and admired the house they had just built.
     H The volunteers were filled with pride, stepping back to admire the house they had just built.
     J The house they had just built filled the volunteers with pride, so they stepped back and admired it.

11 **A** Calling the box office, Catherine wasn't sure what time the movie started.
     B Catherine wasn't sure what time the movie started, so she called the box office.
     C Because she called the box office, Catherine wasn't sure what time the movie started.
     D Although she wasn't sure what time the movie started, Catherine called the box office.

Lydia's report about technology continues here. Use it to do numbers 12-15.

Many forms of technology were used for a
(1)

different purpose before their most powerful

application was discovered. The button, for
(2)

example. It was used as an ornament before someone
(3)

discovered that a button and a hole could fasten

clothing quite well. Another example is the wheel.
(4)

For centuries, it was used horizontally to make
(5)

pottery. Someone eventually turned a wheel on its
(6)

side and changed history in an instant. A third
(7)

example is writing it was invented to record

business transactions long before anyone thought to

use it to record spoken words.

12 Which of these is a run-on?

F 1
G 4
H 6
J 7

13 How can sentences 5 and 6 best be combined without changing their meaning?

A For centuries, it was used horizontally to make pottery until someone eventually turned a wheel on its side and changed history in an instant.

B It eventually turned on its side and changed history in an instant, before having been used to make pottery.

C Having been used to make pottery for centuries, the wheel was turned on its side, eventually changing history.

D History was changed in an instant after centuries of using a wheel to make pottery, someone eventually turned it on its side.

14 How is sentence 1 best written?

F Many forms of technology, which were used for one purpose, before their most powerful application was discovered.

G Before their most powerful application was discovered, many forms of technology they were used for one purpose.

H Before their most powerful application, it was discovered, many forms of technology were used for a different purpose.

J As it is

15 Which group of words is *not* a complete sentence?

A 2
B 3
C 4
D 5

72

STOP

Example   Directions: Read the directions for each section. Fill in the circle for the answer you think is correct.

Read the paragraph below. Find the best topic sentence for the paragraph.

A _____ . She had painted for more than sixty years, but had shown her work to no one other than her husband. A friend had discovered her paintings accidentally and insisted that Mrs. McClellan show them. At the age of seventy-eight, she was having her first art show.

    A Art is often a very private thing.

    B It was one of the proudest moments of Mrs. McClellan's life.

    C Talent emerges in some people very late in life.

    D Mrs. McClellan had always lived what she considered to be a normal life.

Remember, a paragraph should focus on one idea. The correct answer is the one that fits best with the rest of the paragraph.

If you are sure you know which answer choice is correct, mark your answer and move on to the next item.

Practice

Read the paragraph below. Find the best topic sentence for the paragraph.

1 _____ . She would prove to be one of the longest-lived sovereigns in the history of the world. Under Victoria's rule, the British empire spread around the globe, making it the world's first superpower.

    A In 1837, Queen Victoria assumed the throne of England.

    B England has had some remarkable rulers, from Henry VIII to Victoria.

    C The Victorian Period was named after a queen of England.

    D A queen is often, but not always, simply a figurehead.

Find the answer choice that best develops the topic sentence below.

2 Mountain biking is fast becoming a national craze.

    F The sport started in Colorado or California, depending on your source of information. A mountain bike may cost more than one thousand dollars.

    G Many ski areas offer mountain biking in the summer. You take a chair up and ride down.

    H Millions of people around the country enjoy mountain biking everywhere from New York's Central Park to California's Sierra Mountains. Consumers seem to love these go-anywhere bikes with fat tires, a sturdy frame, and twenty-one gears.

    J A mountain bike looks clunkier than a touring bike. The sturdy frame and knobby tires, however, make a mountain bike an all-terrain vehicle. Even with twenty-one gears, it is still hard work pedaling up a steep hill.

For numbers 3 and 4, read the paragraph. Find the sentence that does not belong in the paragraph.

3   1. Plants grow in the most unusual places.   2. Everyone, for example, has probably seen a determined weed poking through an asphalt street.   3. More observant people might have noticed an occasional berry bush growing in the crotch of a tree.   4. Home gardeners grow plants in their own backyards.

A Sentence 1

B Sentence 2

C Sentence 3

D Sentence 4

4   1. A Small Craft Advisory is a warning issued by the National Weather Service. 2. The National Weather Service is an agency of the federal government.   3. It may include winds from 18 to 33 knots.   4. In addition, dangerous waves may form, posing a hazard to small boats.

F Sentence 1

G Sentence 2

H Sentence 3

J Sentence 4

For numbers 5 and 6, read the paragraph. Find the sentence that best fits the blank in the paragraph.

5   For many people, the beginning of spring is marked by the opening of trout season. _____ . There they huddle shoulder to shoulder with other fishing enthusiasts. Most of the anglers never catch a fish, but they still enjoy celebrating the end of winter with their comrades.

A In some states, however, it is legal to fish for trout all year long.

B Fishing for trout has a long history and has been the subject of many books.

C The most popular varieties of trout are brook, brown, and rainbow.

D On this long-awaited day, anglers arise long before dawn and head to their favorite stream.

6   Learning a language other than English is becoming more important. In today's global marketplace, anyone who speaks more than one language is at an advantage. _____. In addition, they will be more likely to advance and be offered opportunities for international travel.

F Job seekers have an easier time finding work if they know a second language.

G Languages that use the Latin alphabet are usually easier to learn.

H More languages are taught in schools today than twenty years ago.

J Home-study courses are one way that people learn a second language.

74

GO

ANSWER ROWS   **3** Ⓐ Ⓑ Ⓒ Ⓓ   **4** Ⓕ Ⓖ Ⓗ Ⓙ   **5** Ⓐ Ⓑ Ⓒ Ⓓ   **6** Ⓕ Ⓖ Ⓗ Ⓙ

For numbers 7-9, use the paragraph below to answer the questions.

> [1]The sun, which is a star, is at the center of the solar system. [2]Nine planets, including the earth, revolve around the sun. [3]The planets also rotate on their own axes. [4]Between the planets Mars and Jupiter are smaller bodies called asteroids that may be the remains of a planet that disintegrated in the distant past. [5]Comets occasionally pass through the solar system but are not considered part of it.

7 **Choose the best opening sentence to add to this paragraph.**

A A planet and a star are different in many ways.
B Our galaxy contains many millions of stars.
C The earth is the third planet from the sun.
D The earth is part of a cluster of objects called the solar system.

8 **Which sentence should be left out of this paragraph?**

F Sentence 1
G Sentence 2
H Sentence 3
J Sentence 4

9 **Where is the best place for sentence 5?**

A Where it is now
B Between sentences 1 and 2
C Between sentences 2 and 3
D Before sentence 1

10 **Which of the following would be most appropriate at the beginning of a report on the Boston Tea Party?**

F Because of their association with Great Britain, colonists in America drank a lot of tea. It was a great inconvenience when the British gave the East India Company a monopoly on tea importation and allowed them to control the price.

G On December 16, 1773, a group of patriots in Boston climbed aboard several ships in the harbor and threw bales of tea overboard. This seemingly insignificant act proved to be one of the earliest skirmishes in the Revolutionary War.

H The Boston Tea Party established Massachusetts as a center of resistance against British rule. It led to the Coercive Acts of 1774, which were intended to penalize Massachusetts and the city of Boston for harboring revolutionaries.

J The Revolutionary War between Britain and her colonies did not happen all at once. For more than ten years before shots were fired at Lexington and Concord, minor skirmishes took place all over the colonies, especially in the colony of Massachusetts.

GO ▷

Here is more of Lydia's report about technology. Use the story to do numbers 11-14.

People in previous centuries were not as
(1)
uninformed as we might think. A calculating
(2)
machine, the forerunner of the computers that help

scientists design and guide rockets, was created by

Charles Babbage in 1823. Consider the rockets that
(3)
are sent into space almost daily. The basis of this
(4)
technology is the invention of gunpowder by the

Chinese around 1000 A.D. The telescopes we use to
(5)
observe rockets in flight owe their development to

Dutch opticians around 1600 A.D. These and
(6)
countless other developments were the building

blocks of the technologies we use every day.

11 **Which sentence could be added before sentence 1?**

  A Technology ranges in size from the smallest computer chip to the largest rocket.
  B Some of today's most advanced technologies had their roots hundreds of years ago.
  C Different civilizations developed different technologies.
  D Very few areas of life have been unaffected by technology.

12 **Which sentence is *not* in the correct place?**

  F 1
  G 2
  H 3
  J 4

13 **What supporting information could be added before sentence 6?**

  A Eye glasses and telescopes are based on similar technology.
  B Their gunpowder was made of charcoal, sulfur, and potassium nitrate.
  C The two kinds of telescopes are those that use lenses and those that use mirrors.
  D The telescope itself was invented in 1608 by the Dutch scientist Johann Lippershey.

14 **Which sentence does *not* belong in the story?**

  F 1
  G 3
  H 5
  J 6

76

STOP

E1

Find the underlined part that is the simple predicate (verb) of the sentence.

An excited crowd of supporters awaited the return of the governor.
    A   B   C   D

For number 1, choose the word or phrase that best completes the sentence.

1   _____ will arrive at the party a little late because we must pick up Alonso.

  A I and her

  B I and she

  C She and I

  D She and me

For number 2, choose the answer that is a complete and correctly written sentence.

2 **F** The grass is growing more slower because there has been so little rain.

  G Our new lawn mower is quietest than the old one.

  H The lid to the gas can was on more tighter so I couldn't loosen it.

  J A loose bolt rattled whenever the lawn mower was started.

For numbers 3-5, read each answer choice. Fill in the space for the choice that has a usage error. If there is no mistake, fill in the fourth answer space.

3 **A** We had to paint the walls
    B twicte since the first coat
    C didn't cover very well.
    D *(No mistakes)*

4 **F** The price of gasoline is high
    G because both the state and federal
    H governments tax it so much.
    J *(No mistakes)*

5 **A** We wanted to go riding yesterday, but
    B catching the horses were a lot
    C harder than we thought it would be.
    D *(No mistakes)*

For number 6, find the underlined part that is the simple subject of the sentence.

6 This afternoon the principal will visit our classroom for an hour.
          F   G   H   J

For number 7, find the underlined part that is the simple predicate (verb) of the sentence.

7 Lewis and his sister climbed the stairs to their apartment on the fifth floor.
    A   B   C   D

GO

For numbers 8-10, choose the answer that best combines the underlined sentences.

8   Almost everyone rode the roller coaster.

Ellen didn't because of her injured hand.

F   Ellen didn't ride the roller coaster, and almost everyone else did, because of her injured hand.
G   Almost everyone rode the roller coaster except Ellen, who didn't because of her injured hand.
H   Almost everyone, except Ellen because of her injured hand, rode the roller coaster.
J   Ellen, who didn't ride the roller coaster because of her injured hand, and everyone else did.

9   Your sister was here earlier.

Your sister left this package for you.

A   Your sister, who was here earlier, left this package for you.
B   Because she was here earlier, your sister left this package for you.
C   Your sister left this package for you and was here earlier.
D   Although she was here earlier, she left this package for you.

10   The library is on the first floor.

The library is at the end of the hall.

The computer center is in the library.

F   The library, which is on the first floor, is at the end of the hall, and the computer center is in it.
G   The computer center, which is in the library, and the library is on the first floor at the end of the hall.
H   The library, although it is at the end of the hall, is on the first floor, and the computer center is in it.
J   The computer center is in the library, which is on the first floor at the end of the hall.

For numbers 11 and 12, choose the best way of expressing the idea.

11   A   The kind of bicycle you want is not in the store, although they have them.
B   The store has bicycles, although not the kind you want.
C   The store, which has bicycles, although not the kind you want.
D   Although not the kind of bicycle you want, the store has them.

12   F   Because they were in the distance, the pioneers would have to cross the huge mountains.
G   Huge mountains were in the distance, although the pioneers would have to cross them.
H   In the distance were the huge mountains that the pioneers would have to cross.
J   Huge mountains, in the distance, and the pioneers would have to cross them.

Read the paragraph below. Find the best topic sentence for the paragraph.

13 _____ . The most common way is when the earth's crust shifts, causing the surface to buckle upward. A less common way of forming mountains is through volcanic action. Both types of mountains are found in the United States.

   A Mountains are formed in one of two ways.

   B Volcanoes are among the most powerful forces of nature.

   C The earth is not as stable as you might think.

   D Humans were not around when most of the earth's mountains were formed.

Find the answer choice that best develops the topic sentence.

14 In some homes, it is necessary to install a water softening appliance.

   F In large cities, homes receive their water from a central source like a lake or reservoir. In more rural areas, homes have their own wells.

   G Water often contains minerals that make the water "hard." The amount of dissolved minerals varies from place to place.

   H It is usually connected to the water supply where it enters the house. Pipes carrying water must be buried far enough underground so they don't freeze.

   J The purpose of this appliance is to remove dissolved minerals from the water supply. These minerals are not harmful, but they prevent soap from forming a good lather.

Read the paragraph below. Find the sentence that does not belong in the paragraph.

15 1. Both the sun and moon exert a strong influence over the earth. 2. This influence is most obvious in large bodies of water. 3. The oceans are the largest bodies of water. 4. The gravitational attraction of the sun and moon cause the tides, which are bulges in these bodies of water.

   A Sentence 1

   B Sentence 2

   C Sentence 3

   D Sentence 4

Read the paragraph below. Find the sentence that best fits the blank in the paragraph.

16 Farming in the United States is undergoing a radical change. _____. The size of these farms, however, is increasing. In addition, fewer farms are owned by families and more are owned by large businesses.

   F Larger farms are usually more profitable than smaller farms.

   G The number of working farms is decreasing each year.

   H This is not the first time in history such a change has taken place.

   J Soybeans are one of the most profitable and useful crops.

GO

Below is the conclusion of Lydia's report about the history of technology. Read the conclusion and use it to do numbers 17-20.

The pace of technological advances faster
(1)
throughout history. This means that the time
(2)
between advancements has got small. The potter's
(3)
wheel, for example, was invented about 3500 B.C. It
(4)
took more than a thousand years for the wheel to be

turned over and used for vehicles. Electricity was
(5)
first produced by Alessandro Volta in 1800. In less
(6)
than a hundred years, electric lights, motors, and

other devices had been created. In other words,
(7)
technological advances are occurring more rapidly

today than in the past. This trend is expected to
(8)
continue in the future. Considering the rapid
(9)
acceleration of technological advancements, who

knows what the world of tomorrow will be like.

17 In sentence 2, <u>has got small</u> is best written —

A has gotten smallest
B gets smallest
C has gotten smaller
D As it is

18 How is sentence 4 best written?

F More than a thousand years passed; however the wheel was turned over and used for vehicles.
G The wheel was not used for vehicles, until more than a thousand years.
H More than a thousand years, it took, for the wheel to be turned over and used for vehicles.
J As it is

19 Which of these sentences would best follow sentence 6?

A Within another twenty years, electricity was being used for hundreds of purposes.
B Today, electrical appliances are found in every home.
C Electricity was far from the last great discovery.
D After electricity was created, other advancements soon took place.

20 Which group of words is <u>not</u> a complete sentence?

F 1
G 4
H 6
J 7

80

ANSWER ROWS   **17** Ⓐ Ⓑ Ⓒ Ⓓ   **18** Ⓕ Ⓖ Ⓗ Ⓙ   **19** Ⓐ Ⓑ Ⓒ Ⓓ   **20** Ⓕ Ⓖ Ⓗ Ⓙ   NUMBER RIGHT _____

Lesson 8   Spelling Skills

Examples   **Directions:** Follow the directions for each section. Choose the answer you think is correct.

Find the word that is spelled correctly and fits best in the blank.	Choose the phrase in which the underlined word is **not** spelled correctly.
A What time will be _____ for you?	**B** **F** <u>benefit</u> show
A convenent	**G** <u>surfase</u> area
B convienient	**H** correctly <u>multiply</u>
C convenint	**J** sticky <u>residue</u>
D convenient	

Tips

Read the directions carefully. Be sure you know if you should look for the correctly spelled word or the incorrectly spelled word.

Remember, words that look familiar are usually spelled right. Words that look strange are usually spelled wrong.

Practice

For numbers 1-5, find the word that is spelled correctly and fits best in the blank.

1   The bell caused a _____ of activity.

  A   flurry
  B   flurrie
  C   flury
  D   flurrey

2   Were you able to _____ the controls?

  F   mannipulate
  G   manipulait
  H   manipulate
  J   menipulate

3   Annie made a _____ argument.

  A   pursuasive
  B   persuasive
  C   perswasive
  D   purswasive

4   The discovery proved to be _____ .

  F   significent
  G   significant
  H   significint
  J   signifigant

5   _____ art can be hard to understand.

  A   Abstrak
  B   Abstrect
  C   Abstract
  D   Abbstract

For numbers 6-8, read the phrases. Choose the phrase in which the underlined word is **not** spelled correctly.

6   **F**   <u>cautious</u> approach
    G   friendly <u>quarrel</u>
    H   <u>bisect</u> an angle
    J   loud <u>disturbence</u>

7   **A**   daily <u>routene</u>
    B   clever <u>detective</u>
    C   <u>amusement</u> park
    D   <u>inspire</u> confidence

8   **F**   minor <u>annoyance</u>
    G   <u>optimistic</u> attitude
    H   mild <u>symptum</u>
    J   <u>impressive</u> showing

GO

ANSWER ROWS   **A** Ⓐ Ⓑ Ⓒ Ⓓ   **1** Ⓐ Ⓑ Ⓒ Ⓓ   **3** Ⓐ Ⓑ Ⓒ Ⓓ   **5** Ⓐ Ⓑ Ⓒ Ⓓ   **7** Ⓐ Ⓑ Ⓒ Ⓓ
             B Ⓕ Ⓖ Ⓗ Ⓙ   **2** Ⓕ Ⓖ Ⓗ Ⓙ   **4** Ⓕ Ⓖ Ⓗ Ⓙ   **6** Ⓕ Ⓖ Ⓗ Ⓙ   **8** Ⓕ Ⓖ Ⓗ Ⓙ

81

For numbers 9-11, read each answer. Fill in the space for the choice that has a spelling error. If there is no mistake, fill in the last answer space.

9 **A** hectic
    B overlap
    C novise
    D prominent
    E *(No mistakes)*

10 **F** encoureged
    G insulted
    H peasant
    J tributaries
    K *(No mistakes)*

11 **A** methodical
    B wrinkle
    C baffled
    D departure
    E *(No mistakes)*

For numbers 12-14, read each phrase. One of the underlined words is not spelled correctly for the way it is used in the phrase. Fill in the space for the word that is **not** spelled correctly.

12 **F** invading <u>horde</u>
    G <u>scent</u> of roses
    H dinner <u>role</u>
    J sharp <u>angle</u>

13 **A** <u>nominations</u> for president
    B sharp <u>all</u>
    C <u>stir</u> soup
    D <u>wrap</u> a package

14 **F** <u>vague</u> answer
    G hungry <u>calf</u>
    H <u>bread</u> horses
    J orange <u>grove</u>

For numbers 15-18, find the underlined part that is misspelled. If all the words are spelled correctly, mark the space under <u>No mistake</u>.

15 Your <u>conduckt</u> during the <u>emergency</u> was <u>heroic</u>. <u>No mistake.</u>
           A   **B**   **C**   **D**

16 The <u>signature</u> on the <u>document</u> is <u>authentec</u>. <u>No mistake.</u>
        F   **G**   **H**   **J**

17 Try to avoid <u>repetitious</u> ideas when you <u>compose</u> your <u>article</u>. <u>No mistake.</u>
               A   **B**   **C**   **D**

18 My mother had to <u>lengthin</u> the <u>gown</u> because I had <u>grown</u> so rapidly. <u>No mistake.</u>
                   F   **G**   **H**   **J**

Example   **Directions:** For E1, mark the answer choice that is spelled correctly and fits best in the blank. For E2, look for the underlined word that has a spelling mistake. Mark your answer.

E1

New kitchen _____ are expensive.

A apliances
B aplliances
C applianses
D appliances

E2

F feel refreshed

G entertain friends

H clear indacation

J hazardous area

For numbers 1-6, find the word that is spelled correctly and fits best in the blank.

1   _____ is the mark of a good athlete.

A Consistency
B Consistincy
C Consistancy
D Consistencey

2   What is the _____ of that elevator?

F capasity
G capacity
H capacitie
J capasitey

3   A gas furnace is very _____ .

A ifficient
B effecient
C effecent
D efficient

4   Terry _____ the charcoal.

F ignighted
G ignitted
H igknighted
J ignited

5   The auto mechanic seemed very _____ .

A compitint
B competent
C compitent
D competint

6   The town was _____ by the storm.

F devistated
G devastitated
H devastated
J devastatated

For numbers 7-10, read the phrases. Choose the phrase in which the underlined word is **not** spelled correctly.

7 A seem arrogent

   B probable cause

   C good salary

   D hasty decision

8 F we concurr

   G assist them

   H slight fracture

   J hesitate briefly

9 A feel obliged

   B narrow margin

   C saluted sharply

   D gas guage

10 F repel insects

   G attentive audience

   H show integerity

   J prosperous decade

GO ⟩

ANSWER ROWS   **E1** Ⓐ Ⓑ Ⓒ Ⓓ   **2** Ⓕ Ⓖ Ⓗ Ⓙ   **5** Ⓐ Ⓑ Ⓒ Ⓓ   **8** Ⓕ Ⓖ Ⓗ Ⓙ
  E2 Ⓕ Ⓖ Ⓗ Ⓙ   **3** Ⓐ Ⓑ Ⓒ Ⓓ   **6** Ⓕ Ⓖ Ⓗ Ⓙ   **9** Ⓐ Ⓑ Ⓒ Ⓓ
  1 Ⓐ Ⓑ Ⓒ Ⓓ   **4** Ⓕ Ⓖ Ⓗ Ⓙ   **7** Ⓐ Ⓑ Ⓒ Ⓓ   **10** Ⓕ Ⓖ Ⓗ Ⓙ

83

For numbers 11-13, read each answer. Fill in the space for the choice that has a spelling error. If there is no mistake, fill in the last answer space.

11 A aggressive
    B fertilize
    C delighted
    D mancion
    E *(No mistakes)*

12 F circumstance
    G inaccurate
    H revarence
    J encounter
    K *(No mistakes)*

13 A tantalyze
    B familiar
    C misfortune
    D astounding
    E *(No mistakes)*

For numbers 14-16, read each phrase. One of the underlined words is not spelled correctly for the way it is used in the phrase. Fill in the space for the word that is <u>not</u> spelled correctly.

14 F <u>petty</u> complaint
    G fishing <u>lure</u>
    H <u>slender</u> tree
    J <u>pore</u> showing

15 A <u>vocal</u> group
    B large <u>tract</u>
    C <u>steal</u> beams
    D seem <u>bored</u>

16 F mountain <u>peek</u>
    G be <u>certain</u>
    H <u>crisp</u> lettuce
    J rapidly <u>pursue</u>

For numbers 17-20, find the underlined part that is misspelled. If all the words are spelled correctly, mark the space under <u>No mistake</u>.

17 <u>Shortsited</u> people <u>waste</u> their time and other <u>resources.</u> <u>No mistake.</u>
         A   B   C   D

18 <u>Several</u> of the <u>contributers</u> to the paper were from the <u>debating</u> club. <u>No mistake.</u>
        F   G   H   J

19 We <u>registered</u> for an <u>excersion</u> into the redwood <u>forest.</u> <u>No mistake.</u>
           A   B   C   D

20 The <u>decision</u> was <u>rendered</u> by an <u>impartial</u> judge. <u>No mistake.</u>
          F   G   H   J

Example   **Directions:** Follow the directions for each section. Choose the answer you think is correct.

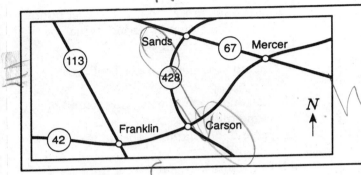

A Look at the map on the left. What direction would you go to travel from Sands to Carson?

A North
B South
C East
D West

If you are not sure which answer choice is correct, try this strategy. Read the question, look at the illustration if there is one, and then look at the answer choices. If necessary, read the question again. Then try to find the right answer.

Practice

Use this table comparing cordless telephones to answer numbers 1 and 2.

CORDLESS TELEPHONES

MODELS	FEATURES					
	Channels	Noise Filter	Replaceable Battery	Memory Dial	Redial	Switchable Tone/Pulse
Anderson	10	•		10	•	•
Danson	2	•	•		•	•
Granville	6		•	10	•	•
Kingsley	10			6	•	•
Orson	6	•		10	•	•
Ranyo	10		•	6	•	•
Sotay	2	•			•	•
TransBand	10	•	•	10	•	•

1 How many phones have noise filters?

A 2
B 3
C 5
D 8

2 Which phone has the most features?

F TransBand
G Anderson
H Ranyo
J Granville

GO

This application form is for students to complete if they want a summer job. Use the form to do numbers 3-5.

```
┌─────────────────────────────────────────┐
│              APPLICATION                 │
│  1. Name _____ │
│  2. Address _____  │
│  3. City/State/Zip _____  │
│  4. Telephone _____  │
│  5. Desired Position _____  │
│  6. Desired Salary _____  │
│  7. Experience _____  │
│     _____  │
│     _____  │
│     _____  │
│  8. References (List three. Provide each  │
│     person's name and a daytime phone     │
│     number.)                              │
│     _____  │
│     _____  │
│     _____  │
└─────────────────────────────────────────┘
```

3 Suppose you were interested in a job as an assistant gardener. On which line would you write this job?

    A Line 1   **C** Line 5
    B Line 2   **D** Line 6

4 What should you write on line 8?

    F the names of people who know what kind of job you can do
    G the names of your family members
    H the names of the people with whom you want to work
    J the names of your classmates

5 Where would you show that you had worked part-time for a year at a garden center?

    A Line 5
    B Line 6
    C Line 7
    D Line 8

Read each question below. Mark the space for the answer you think is correct.

6 Suppose you wanted to use an exact quote by Karen Blixen about Africa. Which of these methods would you use?

    F Include the name of her book in the bibliography.
    G Use quotation marks and include her name in the glossary.
    H Include her name in the table of contents and index.
    J Use quotation marks and indicate where you got the quote.

7 For which reason would you use a thesaurus?

    A to find a synonym for a common word you feel you have overused
    B to find the definition of a word whose meaning you are unsure of
    C to find the pronunciation of a word you are not sure how to say
    D to find a word that rhymes with a word you have already used

8 Pete wants to write a story about everyday life in the American West during the 1800s. Which of these would provide the best picture of everyday life then?

    F a description of what happens when a large gold strike is discovered
    G a description of how Rachel, a 12-year old girl, spends her days
    H a description of how a young man escaped from a gang of robbers
    J a description of how a family survived being lost in the desert

STOP

ANSWER ROWS
3 Ⓐ Ⓑ Ⓒ Ⓓ   5 Ⓐ Ⓑ Ⓒ Ⓓ   7 Ⓐ Ⓑ Ⓒ Ⓓ
4 Ⓕ Ⓖ Ⓗ Ⓙ   6 Ⓕ Ⓖ Ⓗ Ⓙ   8 Ⓕ Ⓖ Ⓗ Ⓙ

86

Examples   Directions: Read the question. Mark the answer you think is correct.

E1

In a textbook, where would you find the year that the book was published?

A   the index
B   the bibliography
C   the back of the title page
D   the table of contents

E2

Which of these would you most likely find in the index of a science book?

F   solar power, 227-256
G   Technology Publishing, Dallas
H   Jupiter: the largest of the planets
J   Chapter 23, Fiber Optics

Study the magazine table of contents below. Use it to do numbers 1-4.

Boating Today

Cover: Sailing under Philadelphia's Ben Franklin Bridge
Photography by Nelson Hunter

2   **From the Editor:** Boating Safety on Crowded Waters

3   **Letters to the Editor**

6   **City Waters**
Boating adventures in five large cities
by Kate Warnock

10   **Rivers to the Sea**
Navigating small boats in tricky currents
by Will Marley

17   **In-season Maintenance**
Keeping your craft in tip-top shape while you enjoy it
by Kip and Mary Teeter

20   **Canyons of Blue**
Utah's Lake Powell is hard to reach but worth the effort
by Ida Gonzales

27   **Update:** Is the new law in Texas working?
by Jean Shields

32   **End of Issue**
Things they never told you when you bought your boat
by Karen Anderson

---

1   On which page would you find letters written from readers to the editor of the magazine?

A   Page 1
B   Page 2
C   Page 3
D   Page 27

2   On which page does an article begin that relates to the picture on the cover of the magazine?

F   Page 6
G   Page 10
H   Page 17
J   Page 32

3   Which of these might be found on page 23?

A   a road map showing how to get to Chicago
B   a discussion of a new product to protect a boat's hull
C   a list of places where boating is hazardous
D   a road map showing how to get to Lake Powell

4   Who wrote about a hard-to-reach lake?

F   Karen Anderson
G   Will Marley
H   Nelson Hunter
J   Ida Gonzales

The map below shows an imaginary continent named Natara and a nearby island, Orad Island. Use the map to answer numbers 5-8.

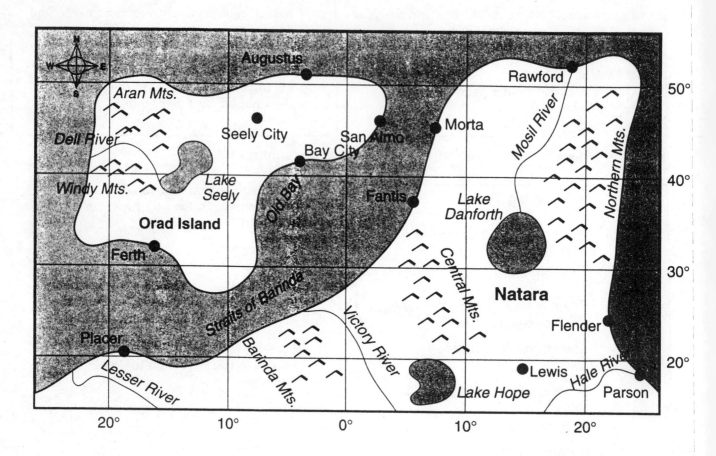

5 Which city is at 53° N, 18° E?

   A Augustus
   B Flender
   C Ferth
   D Rawford

6 Where is the Dell River?

   F east of Lake Seely
   G between the Aran and Windy Mountains
   H south of the Central Mountains
   J between the Central Mountains and Victory River

7 Which city on Orad Island is closest to Morta?

   A San Almo
   B Bay City
   C Augustus
   D Fantis

8 Which city is on the east coast of Natara and not on a river?

   F Parson
   G Fantis
   H Flender
   J Placer

GO

ANSWER ROWS   **5** Ⓐ Ⓑ Ⓒ Ⓓ   **7** Ⓐ Ⓑ Ⓒ Ⓓ
   6 Ⓕ Ⓖ Ⓗ Ⓙ   **8** Ⓕ Ⓖ Ⓗ Ⓙ

In order to use reference materials, you must choose a word or phrase with which to search. For numbers 9-11, select the best word or phrase to answer the question.

9   Which key term should you use to find information about the depth and area of the Atlantic Ocean?

A   Ocean
B   Atlantic Ocean
C   Depth and Area
D   World Oceans

10   Wind is caused by unequal heating of the earth's surface. Which term should you use to find more information about one of the most severe forms of wind, the tornado?

F   Wind
G   Heating
H   Severe
J   Tornado

11   Which key term should you use to find information about the advantages and disadvantages of using planes, trains, or trucks to transport manufactured products?

A   Plane
B   Train
C   Transportation
D   Manufactured Products

For numbers 12-14, choose the word that would appear first if the words were arranged in alphabetical order.

12   F   subacute
     G   subalpine
     H   subculture
     J   subbing

13   A   consort
     B   conspire
     C   console
     D   conspiracy

14   F   mastic
     G   masthead
     H   mastoid
     J   mastodon

For numbers 15 and 16, choose the important phrase that should be included in research notes on city planning.

15   A well-designed city should allow residents to live, work, and play easily, while at the same time it should be safe and attractive.

A   cities should be well-designed to allow residents
B   cities should be convenient for residents, safe, attractive
C   residents allowed to live, work, play in city
D   well-designed by residents for convenient cities

16   Parks should be placed so they are convenient and inviting, with both open spaces for play and secluded areas where residents can escape the hubbub of the city.

F   convenient and inviting parks with open and secluded spaces
G   parks for residents in secluded areas or open spaces
H   inviting residents to open spaces or secluded areas
J   residents can escape to open spaces in a park

STOP

ANSWER ROWS   9 Ⓐ Ⓑ Ⓒ Ⓓ   11 Ⓐ Ⓑ Ⓒ Ⓓ   13 Ⓐ Ⓑ Ⓒ Ⓓ   15 Ⓐ Ⓑ Ⓒ Ⓓ
              10 Ⓕ Ⓖ Ⓗ Ⓙ   12 Ⓕ Ⓖ Ⓗ Ⓙ   14 Ⓕ Ⓖ Ⓗ Ⓙ   16 Ⓕ Ⓖ Ⓗ Ⓙ   NUMBER RIGHT _____

To the Student:

These tests will give you a chance to put the tips you have learned to work.

A few last reminders…

- Be sure you understand all the directions before you begin each test. You may ask the teacher questions about the directions if you do not understand them.
- Work as quickly as you can during each test.
- When you change an answer, be sure to erase your first mark completely.

- You can guess at an answer or skip difficult items and go back to them later.
- Use the tips you have learned whenever you can.
- It is OK to be a little nervous. You may even do better.

Now that you have completed the lessons in this unit, you are on your way to scoring high!

STUDENT'S NAME		SCHOOL
LAST	FIRST	MI	TEACHER

FEMALE ○   MALE ○

BIRTHDATE

MONTH	DAY	YEAR

GRADE ⑦ ⑧ ⑨

PART 1   LANGUAGE MECHANICS

E1 Ⓐ Ⓑ Ⓒ Ⓓ	**4** Ⓕ Ⓖ Ⓗ Ⓙ	**8** Ⓕ Ⓖ Ⓗ Ⓙ	**12** Ⓕ Ⓖ Ⓗ Ⓙ	**16** Ⓕ Ⓖ Ⓗ Ⓙ	**19** Ⓐ Ⓑ Ⓒ Ⓓ
1 Ⓐ Ⓑ Ⓒ Ⓓ	**5** Ⓐ Ⓑ Ⓒ Ⓓ	**9** Ⓐ Ⓑ Ⓒ Ⓓ	**13** Ⓐ Ⓑ Ⓒ Ⓓ	**17** Ⓐ Ⓑ Ⓒ Ⓓ	**20** Ⓕ Ⓖ Ⓗ Ⓙ
2 Ⓕ Ⓖ Ⓗ Ⓙ	**6** Ⓕ Ⓖ Ⓗ Ⓙ	**10** Ⓕ Ⓖ Ⓗ Ⓙ	**14** Ⓕ Ⓖ Ⓗ Ⓙ	**18** Ⓕ Ⓖ Ⓗ Ⓙ	**21** Ⓐ Ⓑ Ⓒ Ⓓ
3 Ⓐ Ⓑ Ⓒ Ⓓ	**7** Ⓐ Ⓑ Ⓒ Ⓓ	**11** Ⓐ Ⓑ Ⓒ Ⓓ	**15** Ⓐ Ⓑ Ⓒ Ⓓ		

PART 2   LANGUAGE EXPRESSION

E1 Ⓐ Ⓑ Ⓒ Ⓓ	**4** Ⓕ Ⓖ Ⓗ Ⓙ	**8** Ⓕ Ⓖ Ⓗ Ⓙ	**12** Ⓕ Ⓖ Ⓗ Ⓙ	**15** Ⓐ Ⓑ Ⓒ Ⓓ	**18** Ⓕ Ⓖ Ⓗ Ⓙ
1 Ⓐ Ⓑ Ⓒ Ⓓ	**5** Ⓐ Ⓑ Ⓒ Ⓓ	**9** Ⓐ Ⓑ Ⓒ Ⓓ	**13** Ⓐ Ⓑ Ⓒ Ⓓ	**16** Ⓕ Ⓖ Ⓗ Ⓙ	**19** Ⓐ Ⓑ Ⓒ Ⓓ
2 Ⓕ Ⓖ Ⓗ Ⓙ	**6** Ⓕ Ⓖ Ⓗ Ⓙ	**10** Ⓕ Ⓖ Ⓗ Ⓙ	**14** Ⓕ Ⓖ Ⓗ Ⓙ	**17** Ⓐ Ⓑ Ⓒ Ⓓ	**20** Ⓕ Ⓖ Ⓗ Ⓙ
3 Ⓐ Ⓑ Ⓒ Ⓓ	**7** Ⓐ Ⓑ Ⓒ Ⓓ	**11** Ⓐ Ⓑ Ⓒ Ⓓ			

PART 3   SPELLING

E1 Ⓐ Ⓑ Ⓒ Ⓓ	**3** Ⓐ Ⓑ Ⓒ Ⓓ	**7** Ⓐ Ⓑ Ⓒ Ⓓ	**11** Ⓐ Ⓑ Ⓒ Ⓓ Ⓔ	**15** Ⓐ Ⓑ Ⓒ Ⓓ	**19** Ⓐ Ⓑ Ⓒ Ⓓ
E2 Ⓕ Ⓖ Ⓗ Ⓙ	**4** Ⓕ Ⓖ Ⓗ Ⓙ	**8** Ⓕ Ⓖ Ⓗ Ⓙ	**12** Ⓕ Ⓖ Ⓗ Ⓙ Ⓚ	**16** Ⓕ Ⓖ Ⓗ Ⓙ	**20** Ⓕ Ⓖ Ⓗ Ⓙ
1 Ⓐ Ⓑ Ⓒ Ⓓ	**5** Ⓐ Ⓑ Ⓒ Ⓓ	**9** Ⓐ Ⓑ Ⓒ Ⓓ	**13** Ⓐ Ⓑ Ⓒ Ⓓ Ⓔ	**17** Ⓐ Ⓑ Ⓒ Ⓓ	
2 Ⓕ Ⓖ Ⓗ Ⓙ	**6** Ⓕ Ⓖ Ⓗ Ⓙ	**10** Ⓕ Ⓖ Ⓗ Ⓙ	**14** Ⓕ Ⓖ Ⓗ Ⓙ	**18** Ⓕ Ⓖ Ⓗ Ⓙ	

PART 4   STUDY SKILLS

E1 Ⓐ Ⓑ Ⓒ Ⓓ	**3** Ⓐ Ⓑ Ⓒ Ⓓ	**6** Ⓕ Ⓖ Ⓗ Ⓙ	**9** Ⓐ Ⓑ Ⓒ Ⓓ
1 Ⓐ Ⓑ Ⓒ Ⓓ	**4** Ⓕ Ⓖ Ⓗ Ⓙ	**7** Ⓐ Ⓑ Ⓒ Ⓓ	**10** Ⓕ Ⓖ Ⓗ Ⓙ
2 Ⓕ Ⓖ Ⓗ Ⓙ	**5** Ⓐ Ⓑ Ⓒ Ⓓ	**8** Ⓕ Ⓖ Ⓗ Ⓙ	**11** Ⓐ Ⓑ Ⓒ Ⓓ

Part 1   Language Mechanics

Example   **Directions:** Fill in the answer choice for the punctuation mark that is needed. Choose "None" if no more punctuation is needed in the sentence.

E1

Did the dog bark when you came in

A   .   B   !   C   ?   D   None

---

1   Finally you should remember to wear a hat and use sun screen.

A   :   B   ;   C   ,   **D   None**

2   The gymnasium was packed with the following fans students, parents, and teachers.

F   ;   G   :   H   .   **J   None**

3   "You can wash the windows with vinegar," suggested Norm.

A   :   B   ,   C   ;   **D   None**

4   Russel my cousin, has lived in Michigan for a long time.

F   ,   G   ?   H   :   **J   None**

For numbers 5-7, read each answer. Fill in the space for the choice that has a punctuation error. If there is no mistake, fill in the fourth answer space.

5   A   Sharona got dressed, washed
        B   her face, and brushed her teeth before
        C   coming downstairs for breakfast.
        D   *(No mistakes)*

6   F   "It's no use, Ted muttered."
        G   "No matter what we try, we
        H   still can't get this car started."
        J   *(No mistakes)*

7   A   When I tried to call the
        B   number you gave me I
        C   got a busy signal again and again.
        D   *(No mistakes)*

For numbers 8 and 9, read each sentence with a blank. Choose the word or words that fit best in the blank and show the correct punctuation.

8   The item you ordered will be delivered by _____ shipping will be free.

        F   Tuesday. Or
        G   Tuesday: or
        H   Tuesday, or
        J   Tuesday or,

9   The _____ science projects were set up in the auditorium.

        A   children's
        B   childrens
        C   childrens's
        D   childrens'

GO

For numbers 10-12, read each answer. Fill in the space for the choice that has a capitalization error. If there is no mistake, fill in the fourth answer space.

10 **F**   One of the most important
     G aspects of commerce is selling U.S.
     H goods and services to other Countries.
     J *(No mistakes)*

11 **A**   People who own a house or apartment
     B must spend a lot of time maintaining
     C and improving their property.
     D *(No mistakes)*

12 **F**   My Uncle, Toby Hazlett,
     G is a teacher who is running
     H for office in our county.
     J *(No mistakes)*

For number 13, read each group of sentences. Find the one that is written correctly and shows the correct capitalization and punctuation.

13 **A** Teresa thought for a minute. "I have a suggestion. Lets spend Saturday morning cleaning up the park. Have you seen how much trash is there?

     B "I don't know," answered Chang. "That's a big job, and it will take us all morning. I'm not sure I want to volunteer that much time."

     C "We have all used the Park a zillion times" Argued Pedro. "It's only one Saturday morning, and we'll have fun. We can have a picnic after."

     D Tonie smiled and added, Come on, Chang. You'd just sleep in on Saturday. Meet us at eight oclock at the park. I'll bring my mother's brownies."

For numbers 14-16, read the sentence with a blank. Mark the space beside the answer choice that fits best in the blank and has correct capitalization and punctuation.

14 The manager of our team, _____ makes sure the equipment is ready for our games.

     F Lori Gallagher
     G Lori Gallagher:
     H Lori Gallagher;
     J Lori Gallagher,

15 The highest peak in our county is _____ it is more than 3000 meters high.

     A mt. Sorrel:
     B Mt. Sorrel;
     C Mt. Sorrel
     D Mt Sorrel,

16 The carnival will open on _____ I can't go until Friday.

     F Tuesday but
     G Tuesday. But
     H Tuesday, but
     J Tuesday: but

Choose the correct answer for number 17.

17 Which is the correct way to begin a business letter?

     A Dear Madam:
     B Dear Madam
     C Dear Madam;
     D Dear madam,

GO

Frances is spending the summer with her cousins. This letter is to her parents. Read her letter and use it to do numbers 18-21.

July 4, 1995

Dear Mom and Dad,

I miss <u>you! but</u> not as much as before. How is
   (1)   **(2)**
that big old dog of mine? Is he wondering where I
                        (3)
am? Give him a hug for me.
     (4)

Aunt Rita and Uncle Bill took us to Minneapolis
   (5)
<u>and st. Paul</u> last week. We went shopping, had
                 (6)
dinner, and then went to a baseball game. Watching
                           (7)
the game was <u>great; the</u> Twins, however, didn't win.
Marcie was really bummed. I can't believe she's
                     (8)
such a fan.

I'm reading a book called <u>angle of repose</u>. Uncle
   (9)   **(10)**
Bill said it was the best book ever written. You
                           (11)
know how he exaggerates. He's almost right, though.
             (12)
It is the best book I've ever read.
  (13)

18 In sentence 1, <u>you! but</u> is best written —

F you, but
G you. But
H you but,
J As it is

19 In sentence 5, <u>and st. Paul</u> is best written —

A and St. Paul,
B and St. Paul
C and, St. Paul
D As it is

20 In sentence 7, <u>great; the</u> is best written —

F great the
G great: the
H great. the
J As it is

21 In sentence 9, <u>angle of repose</u> is best written —

A Angle of Repose
B *angle of repose*
C *Angle of Repose*
D As it is

STOP

Example

Directions: Find the underlined part that is the simple predicate (verb) of the sentence.

E1

At last, the weary explorers reached the lake for which they were looking.
          A   B   C   D

For number 1, choose the word or phrase that best completes the sentence.

1   The newspaper _____ a list of students who made the honor roll.

   A   publishing

   B   were published

   C   have published

   D   has published

For number 2, choose the answer that is a complete and correctly written sentence.

2   F   We will all meet this afternoon, at the park beside the school.

   G   If you would like we can meet at your house at two o'clock.

   H   Unless you hurry, you will never catch up with Chad and Maria.

   J   No we will not be able to bring our dogs to the park.

For numbers 3-5, read each answer choice. Fill in the space for the choice that has a usage error. If there is no mistake, fill in the fourth answer space.

3   A   At the banquet tomorrow night,
    B   Lenore will except the award she
    C   received for her volunteer service.
    D   *(No mistakes)*

4   F   An exceptionally large package
    G   arrived for Sal. He has no idea
    H   what it is or who sent it.
    J   *(No mistakes)*

5   A   Before I left for school this morning,
    B   I should of walked the dog. Now
    C   my father will have to do it.
    D   *(No mistakes)*

For number 6, find the underlined part that is the simple subject of the sentence.

6   Even with the bad weather, the crowd was much larger than we expected.
     F   G   H   J

For number 7, find the underlined part that is the simple predicate (verb) of the sentence.

7   Tornadoes occur more often in the United States than in any other country.
             A   B   C   D

GO

For numbers 8-10, choose the answer that best combines the underlined sentences.

8 You can go to the baseball game.

Come home right after it is over.

F You can go, to the baseball game, although you should come home right after it is over.
G You can go to the baseball game, but come home right after it is over.
H Come home right after the game is over, but you can go to it.
J Coming home right after the baseball game, although you can go to it.

9 Let's take a walk after dinner.

Let's walk to the creek.

A Let's take a walk to the creek after dinner.
B After dinner, let's take a walk, and take it to the creek.
C Let's take a walk after dinner, a walk to the creek.
D After dinner, let's take a walk, which is to the creek.

10 Kisha is Mac's sister.

Kisha went to Purdue University.

Purdue University is in Indiana.

F Kisha is Mac's sister, and she went to Purdue University, which is in Indiana.
G Purdue University, which is in Indiana, is where Kisha went, who is Mac's sister.
H Kisha, who is Mac's sister, went to Indiana, where Purdue University is.
J Mac's sister Kisha went to Purdue University, which is in Indiana.

For numbers 11 and 12, choose the best way of expressing the idea.

11 A Although you go to the store, please pick up the things I've written on this list.
B While you go to the store, and please pick up the things I've written on this list.
C When you go to the store, please pick up the things I've written on this list.
D On this list are written things you should pick up, please, when you go to the store.

12 F I really can't, Horace, believe you want to go to school this summer.
G This summer, I really can't believe you want to go to school, Horace.
H Horace, I really can't believe you want to go to school this summer.
J Really, Horace, this summer I can't believe you want to go to school.

Read the paragraph below. Find the best topic sentence for the paragraph.

13 _____ . Some businesses manufacture products such as automobiles, toys, or clothing. Others provide services, such as banking, entertainment, and retail shopping. A few businesses such as telephone companies offer both products and services.

   A Businesses usually fall into one of two categories.

   B One of the benefits of living in the United States is the ability to start a business.

   C Large and small companies have different ways of succeeding.

   D Successful businesses know what their customers want.

Find the answer choice that best develops the topic sentence.

14   Brenda was looking forward to her trip to the ocean.

   F She and her family would fly to Florida. They would spend a week there visiting her aunt and uncle.

   G She had heard all about the ocean from her friend, Steven. He had recently moved from Delaware to Kentucky.

   H Like many other young people who live in Kentucky, she had never seen the ocean. She couldn't imagine what that much water must look like.

   J She had lived in Kentucky her whole life. She enjoyed water sports like swimming, fishing, and boating.

Read the paragraph below. Find the sentence that does not belong in the paragraph.

15   1. Many people believe that the person known as "Calamity Jane" was a fictional character. 2. She was, however, a very real person named Martha Jane Canary.   3. She lived from 1852 to 1903 and was known as an expert with both horses and a six-shooter.   4. The Old West was the home for many interesting characters.

   A Sentence 1

   B Sentence 2

   C Sentence 3

   D Sentence 4

Read the paragraph below. Find the sentence that best fits the blank in the paragraph.

16   An automobile engine works on a simple principle. _____. An electrical spark ignites the mixture of gasoline and air. When the mixture explodes, it forces the piston out of the cylinder so it turns a shaft.

   F Automobile engines have four, six, or eight cylinders.

   G Gasoline and air are mixed in a cylinder with a piston.

   H The engine is connected to a series of gears called the transmission.

   J Gasoline is a substance that is easily ignited.

GO

Below is more of the letter Frances wrote to her parents. Read the letter and use it to do numbers 17-20.

Every Tuesday morning, all of us go to a camp
(1)
for disabled children. They have a horseback riding
(2)
program there, and we are volunteers. I'm learning
(3)
a lot about horses. Did you know that a horse has a
(4)
blind spot right in front of its face? Because a
(5)
horse's eyes are located on the side of its head,

it <u>can't hardly see</u> what is in front of its nose.

The blind spot, caused by the location of the
(6)
horse's eyes, makes the horse turn its head to see.

I'm amazed to see how well so many of the
(7)
children can ride. One little girl can't walk and
(8)
uses a wheel chair. When she gets on a horse,
(9)
although she rides like a champion. She is only
(10)
eight years old and wants to go to the Olympics

some day. Isn't that great?
(11)

17 **Which sentence could be added after sentence 2?**

A There are many different kinds of camps in Minnesota.
B As I am sure you remember, I don't know very much about horses.
C Most of the children at the camp are from Minnesota.
D Aunt Rita and Uncle Bill have done it for several years now.

18 **Which sentence needlessly repeats an idea?**

F 2
G 3
H 6
J 8

19 **How is sentence 9 best written?**

A When she gets on a horse, but she rides like a champion
B When she gets on a horse, however, she rides like a champion.
C She rides like a champion, however, and she gets on a horse.
D As it is

20 **In sentence 5, <u>can't hardly see</u> is best written —**

F can't see
G can't see hardly
H can't not see
J As it is

STOP

Example   Directions: For E1, choose the word that is spelled correctly and fits best in the blank. For E2, choose the phrase in which the underlined word is <u>not</u> spelled correctly.

E1

_____ the town will take three hours.

A Evacuating
B Evacuting
C Evuacuating
D Evaccuating

E2

F write a <u>narrative</u>

G <u>arid</u> land

H <u>protest</u> the decision

J <u>sparcely</u> populated

For numbers 1-6, find the word that is spelled correctly and fits best in the blank.

1 The deer seemed to _____ from nowhere.

A materilize
B materialize
C materealize
D materialise

2 The _____ asked us to take a seat.

F receptionest
G receptionast
H receptionist
J reciptionist

3 Shannon is a _____ performer.

A versatile
B versatil
C versateil
D versatal

4 The workers _____ a good contract.

F negotiated
G negotiatted
H nigotiated
J nigotiatted

5 We decided to _____ the paper.

A discontenue
B discontinnue
C disconttinue
D discontinue

6 The weather was hot but _____ .

F tolirable
G tolerable
H tolerible
J tollerable

For numbers 7-10, read the phrases. Choose the phrase in which the underlined word is <u>not</u> spelled correctly.

7 A become <u>lengthy</u>

B <u>perceptive</u> comment

C <u>spontanious</u> applause

D <u>biased</u> against

8 F achieve <u>prosperaty</u>

G <u>minor</u> incident

H deep <u>cavern</u>

J enjoyable <u>situation</u>

9 A <u>possible</u> conflict

B nicely <u>decorated</u>

C seem <u>inactive</u>

D <u>enirgetic</u> response

10 F neatly <u>organized</u>

G <u>edible</u> fruit

H <u>influentual</u> official

J use a <u>protractor</u>

GO >

For numbers 11-13, read each answer. Fill in the space for the choice that has a spelling error. If there is no mistake, fill in the last answer space.

11   A   strategy
     B   appearance
     C   gallant
     D   convincing
     E   (No mistakes)

12   F   candid
     G   modern
     H   despense
     J   reveal
     K   (No mistakes)

13   A   certafied
     B   tyrant
     C   disintegrate
     D   informal
     E   (No mistakes)

For numbers 14-16, read each phrase. One of the underlined words is not spelled correctly for the way it is used in the phrase. Fill in the space for the word that is <u>not</u> spelled correctly.

14   F   school <u>motto</u>
     G   <u>sow</u> a shirt
     H   <u>assure</u> them
     J   new <u>title</u>

15   A   <u>staid</u> alert
     B   recent <u>issue</u>
     C   too <u>complex</u>
     D   <u>wander</u> around

16   F   design <u>specialist</u>
     G   clever <u>plot</u>
     H   <u>skim</u> milk
     J   lion's <u>main</u>

For numbers 17-20, find the underlined part that is misspelled. If all the words are spelled correctly, mark the space under <u>No mistake</u>.

17   Harry's <u>opinion</u> went <u>contrarie</u> to that of the <u>majority</u>. <u>No mistake.</u>
              A   B   C   D

18   Native Americans learned to <u>cultavate</u> <u>arid</u> <u>regions</u> of the American West. <u>No mistake.</u>
                                   F   G   H   J

19   The <u>cargo</u> was rapidly <u>unloaded</u> from the <u>freigter</u>. <u>No mistake.</u>
            A   B   C   D

20   A <u>legendery</u> soccer player <u>addressed</u> an <u>audience</u> of young players. <u>No mistake.</u>
          F   G   H   J

STOP

Example   Directions: Study the map. Read the question. Mark the answer you think is correct.

E1

Main St. — Central Ave.
1st Ave., 2nd Ave., 3rd Ave.
● LIBRARY

N W E S

On the map on the left, if you were at 2nd and Central, which direction should you go to get to the library?

A Southwest
B Southeast
C Northwest
D Northeast

Study this outline for a report about computer manufacturing. Use it to answer numbers 1-4.

COMPUTER MANUFACTURING

I. Materials
  A. External parts
    1. Cases
    2. Cables
    3. Connectors
  B. Internal parts
    1. Electronics
    2. Power supply
    3. Disk drives
II. _____
  A. Inspect parts
  B. Assemble parts
  C. Test finished parts
    1. Visual inspection
    2. Run test program
    3. _____
III. Warehouse
  A. Package computers
    1. Label accurately
  B. Box and ship
  C. Store safely
IV. Sales
  A. Find new customers
    1. Sell existing products
    2. Develop new product ideas
  B. Follow-up old customers
    1. Check satisfaction
    2. Determine future needs
V. Service
  A. Gain new contracts
    1. Contact clients
    2. Make presentations
  B. Provide service
    1. Troubleshooting
    2. System analysis
    3. Preventive maintenance

1 Line II of the outline is blank. Which of these fits best in the blank?

A Manufacturing
B Pricing
C History of computers
D Advertising

2 Suppose you wanted to add a new heading labeled VI to the outline? Which of these would be most appropriate?

F Computer Chips
G Special Packaging
H Robotic Assembly
J Research and Development

3 Line II.C.3 of the outline is blank. Which of these fits best in the blank?

A Assemble keyboard
B Test in heat and cold
C Ship to customers
D Create new designs

4 How could part III of the outline be improved?

F Add "Visit customers" as part III.D.
G Remove "Box and ship" from the outline
H Make "Store safely" part B and "Box and ship" part C.
J Move "Store safely" from part III to part V.

Use this card from a library card catalog to do numbers 5-8.

622.4

S   **Saunders, Judy**
     Assistive Dogs for Physically
     Challenged Adults / Judy Saunders.
     Edited by Philip Case and Jean Willis.
     Illustrations and photographs by Fritz
     Barnum. Denver: Mountain View
     Publishing Company, 1994.
     256 p.; col. illus.; 24 cm

     1. Assistive dogs   2. Guide dogs
     3. Physically challenged   II. Case,
     Philip   III. Title

---

5   Fritz Barnum is the name of the—

   A author
   B publisher
   C person who provided the illustrations
        and photographs
   D person who trained the assistive dogs for
        the book

6   Which number would be most helpful in
     finding this book in the library?

   F 622.4
   G 256
   H 24
   J 1994

7   In which section of the card catalog would
     this card be found?

   A Title
   B Subject
   C Publisher
   D Author

8   Which of these books would most likely have
     been written by the same author?

   F *The History of Dogs*
   G *Dog Diseases*
   H *Training Guide Dogs for the Blind*
   J *Living Spaces for Challenged Persons*

This is an index from a book about Italy during the Renaissance. Use the index to do numbers 9-11.

INDEX
Page numbers in **bold** type refer to illustrations.

Arno River, water displays on, 19, 282; in flood, 223, 279-280; palaces on, **315**
Bank, Medici, branches of, 34; and the government, 55; decline of, 158-173
Charles V, Holy Roman Emperor, succeeds Emperor Maximilian, 234; takes Milan, 238; marches on Rome, 241, 243-246
Clothes, of 14th century Florence, 21; of 15th century Florence, 22-24; ceremonial attire, **73**; of Roman women, 116-117; of national militia, **211**; uniforms of pages, 268-269
Festivals, pageants, 111; tournaments, **116**; weddings, 280-281
Florence, in 15th century, 19-21; government, 26-28; trade, 33; pageants and festivities, 111, 118-119; wedding customs, 117-118; flood and famine in, 223
Michelangelo Buonarroti (1475-1564), history, 165; his tomb, **312**; his early work, 322; his great works, 389-397
Milan, government of, 27; Florence and, 42, 79-80; Venice and Naples declare war on, 84; Spain and, 219
Savonarola, Girolamo (1452-1498), 178-182; his power in Florence, 191; attitudes toward, 192-193

---

9   Which page would contain a picture of
     clothes worn by the national militia?

   A 21   **C** 73
   B 23   **D** 211

10 Which page would contain a description of
     the government of Florence?

   F 19   **H** 111
   G 27   **J** 117

11 Which page would contain information
     about the relationship of Florence
     and Milan?

   A 24   **C** 78
   B 27   **D** 80

STOP

Table of Contents
Math

UNIT 1   CONCEPTS

Lesson 1   Numeration

Example   **Directions:** Read and work each problem. Find the correct answer. Mark the space for your choice.

A Which of these numbers comes between 95 and 115?

   A 150

   B 105

   C 94

   D 149

B In which of these problems can the dividend be evenly divided by the divisor?

   F 116 ÷ 9

   G 114 ÷ 8

   H 118 ÷ 8

   J 117 ÷ 9

Read each question carefully. Look for key words and numbers that will help you find the answers.

Look at each answer choice before you choose the one you think is correct.

Practice

1 To which value does Arrow A point?

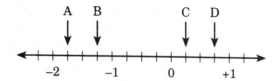

   A $1\frac{1}{2}$

   B $-1\frac{3}{4}$

   C $-1\frac{1}{4}$

   D $-2\frac{1}{4}$

2 What number should replace the □ to make the following a true statement?

$$483,916 = \square + 80,000 + 3000 + 900 + 10 + 6$$

   F 400,000

   G 4,000,000

   H 4

   J 40,000

3 Another way to write 3^5 is —

   A 3 + 5

   B 3 x 5

   C 5 x 5 x 5

   D 3 x 3 x 3 x 3 x 3

4 What number is 10,000 more than 23,971,056?

   F 23,961,056

   G 23,972,056

   H 23,981,056

   J 24,081,056

5 What is the greatest common factor of 39 and 143?

   A 104

   B 13

   C 9

   D 81

GO

6 Which of the number sentences below is <u>false</u>?

F −5 < 0

G −5 > −8

H 4 < −1

J −6 > −10

7 What is the value of the expression in the box?

$$(5 + 3)^2 \div 4$$

A 16

B 2

C 8

D 11

8 One value of $\sqrt{27}$ is between —

F 6 and 7

G 20 and 30

H 2 and 7

J 5 and 6

9 What is the <u>least</u> number that is evenly divisible by 16 and 24?

A 384

B 48

C 64

D 8

10 What is the prime factorization of 75?

F 3 x 25

G 1 x 75

H 3 x 5 x 5

J 3 x 3 x 5

11 $5.09 \times 10^4 =$

A 50,900

B 509

C 5,090,000

D 509,104

12 Which number is between −7 and 5?

F 6

G 9

H −9

J −2

13 Which group of integers is in order from greatest to least?

A 0, 4, 8, 12, 19

B 5, 2, 0, −2, −7

C −6, −2, 0, 19, 14

D −2, 0, 5, 9, 18

14 If 5 motorcycles are as long as 3 cars, what is the smallest number of motorcycles and cars that would be the same length?

F 3 motorcycles and 5 cars

G 50 motorcycles and 30 cars

H 15 motorcycles and 9 cars

J 1 motorcycle and 1 car

15 For the school picture, the students wanted to arrange themselves into lines of 12 each. There weren't enough students, so one line had just 7 students. Which of these could be the number of students?

A 48

B 91

C 120

D 70

STOP

Lesson 2   Number Concepts

Example

Directions: Read and work each problem. Find the correct answer. Mark the space for your choice.

A Six hundred twenty thousand =

   A   60,200

   B   600,200

   C   1620

   D   620,000

B What is 0.28 rounded to the nearest tenth?

   F   0.3

   G   0.1

   H   3.1

   J   0.03

Be sure the answer space you fill in is the same letter as the answer you think is correct.

Key words, numbers, pictures, and figures will help you find the answers.

Practice

1 Which of these is a prime number?

   A 39

   B 75

   C 57

   D 29

2 How much would the value of 825,910 be decreased by replacing the 8 with a 7?

   F   10,000

   G   100,000

   H   1000

   J   1

3 What number goes in the box to make the equation true?

$$3\frac{1}{9} - 1\frac{\square}{9} = 1\frac{2}{9}$$

   A 8

   B 1

   C 13

   D 9

4 Which is the best estimate of $17.88 \times 52\frac{1}{9}$?

   F 15 x 50

   G 20 x 50

   H 15 x 55

   J 20 x 60

5 Look at the number pattern below. What numbers are missing from the pattern?

```
                      3
                 4         4
             7       4         7
         14      8       8       14
     28     16      15      16      28
    —    32      30      30      32     —
```

   A 32 and 48

   B 42 and 42

   C 56 and 56

   D 56 and 32

GO

A Ⓐ Ⓑ Ⓒ Ⓓ   1 Ⓐ Ⓑ Ⓒ Ⓓ   3 Ⓐ Ⓑ Ⓒ Ⓓ   5 Ⓐ Ⓑ Ⓒ Ⓓ

B Ⓕ Ⓖ Ⓗ Ⓙ   2 Ⓕ Ⓖ Ⓗ Ⓙ   4 Ⓕ Ⓖ Ⓗ Ⓙ

6 Using the digits 3, 1, 6, 9, and 8 in two 5-digit numbers, what are the largest and the smallest numbers you can write?

   F 98,163 and 13,986

   G 98,136 and 13,896

   H 98,361 and 13,698

   J 98,631 and 13,689

7 What is 3,287,469 rounded to the nearest ten thousand?

   A 3,280,000

   B 3,010,000

   C 3,290,000

   D 310,000

8 Which of these is <u>not</u> equivalent to $8 \times (9 - 2)$?

   F $(8 \times 9) - (8 \times 2)$

   G 72 - 16

   H $(8 \times 9) - 2$

   J $(9 - 2) \times 8$

9 Look at the number pattern below. One number is missing from the pattern. Which number sentence could be used to find the missing number?

> 1, 3, 5, 9, 15, ___ , 41, 57

   A (15 + 9) + 1

   B (41 - 15) + 1

   C (5 + 9) + 10

   D (57 - 41) + 15

10 How many 2-letter codes can be made from the letters C-A-N if the letters can be repeated in the code? (For example, CC)

   F 12

   G 9

   H 27

   J 6

11 The squares below contain numbers that are related to each other according to the same rule. What number is missing from the third square?

3	6		4	20		2	?
18	2		60	5		42	7

   A 14

   B 9

   C 16

   D 21

12 For a school trip, 56 students went to a museum. All but 11 of the students paid $5.00 to see the video about volcanoes. Which number sentence shows how much the students paid in all to see the video?

   F $(56 + 11) \times 5$

   G $(56 - 11) \times 5$

   H $(56 \times 5) - 11$

   J $(56 - 11) + 5$

13 Which of these is <u>not</u> equal to the others?

   A 65%

   B $\frac{65}{100}$

   C 0.065

   D $6 \div 5$

Example   **Directions:** Read and work each problem. Find the correct answer. Mark the space for your choice.

A 1.05 =

    A $\frac{10}{15}$

    B $\frac{15}{10}$

    C $\frac{100}{105}$

    D $\frac{105}{100}$

B Which of these is greater than the others?

    F two and four tenths

    G nine tenths

    H one and nine tenths

    J two and nine hundredths

Pay close attention to the numbers in the problem and in the answer choices. If you misread even one number, you will probably choose the wrong answer.

If a problem is too difficult, skip it and come back to it later, if you have time.

Practice

1 Which decimal gives the best estimate of the amount of the circle below that is shaded?

    A 0.125

    B 0.40

    C 0.25

    D 0.625

2 Which of these is less than $\frac{4}{9}$?

    F $\frac{1}{3}$

    G $\frac{1}{2}$

    H $\frac{3}{4}$

    J $\frac{5}{8}$

3 What is the reciprocal of $\frac{3}{8}$?

    A $\frac{8}{3}$

    B $\frac{1}{3}$

    C $\frac{1}{8}$

    D $\frac{5}{8}$

4 How would you write 27% as a fraction?

    F $\frac{2}{7}$

    G $\frac{27}{100}$

    H $\frac{.27}{100}$

    J $\frac{17}{10}$

5 Which of these is another name for six and fifteen thousandths?

    A 6.15

    B 6.00015

    C 6015

    D 6.015

GO

ANSWER ROWS   **A** Ⓐ Ⓑ Ⓒ Ⓓ   **1** Ⓐ Ⓑ Ⓒ Ⓓ   **3** Ⓐ Ⓑ Ⓒ Ⓓ   **5** Ⓐ Ⓑ Ⓒ Ⓓ
              B Ⓕ Ⓖ Ⓗ Ⓙ   **2** Ⓕ Ⓖ Ⓗ Ⓙ   **4** Ⓕ Ⓖ Ⓗ Ⓙ

6 Which of these is the simplest name for $\frac{18}{72}$?

   F $\frac{2}{8}$

   G $\frac{4}{35}$

   H $\frac{1}{4}$

   J $\frac{1}{7}$

7 What is another name for $2\frac{2}{9}$?

   A $\frac{29}{2}$

   B $\frac{11}{9}$

   C $\frac{22}{9}$

   D $\frac{20}{9}$

8 What is the least common denominator for $\frac{2}{9}$, $\frac{1}{5}$, and $\frac{4}{15}$?

   F 45

   G 25

   H 27

   J 90

9 What is 0.074 expressed as a percent?

   A 74%

   B 7.4%

   C 0.74%

   D 0.074 %

10 In this number line, P points closest to —

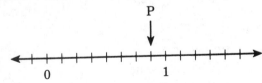

   F 1.12

   G 0.85

   H 0.6

   J 1.6

11 $\frac{3}{16} = \frac{9}{\square}$ $\square =$

   A 48

   B 32

   C 4

   D 3

12 A fisherman wants to buy the lightest sinker he can to hold his bait on the bottom of the lake. Which of these should he buy?

   F $\frac{2}{3}$ ounce

   G $\frac{3}{16}$ ounce

   H $\frac{1}{4}$ ounce

   J $\frac{4}{9}$ ounce

13 Which of these is twenty-three hundredths?

   A 2300

   B 23.001

   C 0.0023

   D 0.23

14 Suppose you wanted to write the numeral 54.085 but forgot the decimal point. How would this change the value of the numeral?

   F It would make it 1000 times smaller.

   G It would make it 1000 times greater.

   H It would make it 100 times greater.

   J It would not change the value.

15 How would you write 0.5% as a decimal?

   A 5.00

   B 0.05

   C 0.005

   D 0.5

STOP

Example   Directions: Read each problem. Mark the answer you think is correct.

E1

If you estimate by rounding to whole numbers, what is 4.8 plus 3.21?

A 5 + 3

B 4 + 3

C 4 + 4

D 3 + 3

E2

What is the greatest common factor of 12, 42, and 54?

F 3

G 7

H 6

J 9

---

1 The absolute value of −41 is —

A $\frac{1}{41}$

B 41

C $\sqrt{41}$

D 41^2

2 6 x 7 − 9 =

F 33

G -12

H 12

J -21

3 Which of these fractions is closest to 0 ?

A $\frac{2}{5}$

B $\frac{1}{12}$

C $\frac{1}{2}$

D $\frac{3}{8}$

4 Which of these is another way to write 4.8 million?

F 48,000,000

G 4,008,000

H 4,080,000

J 4,800,000

5 $5^3 - 50 =$

A 75

B −25

C 3

D 25

6 Which point is at $1\frac{3}{8}$ on this number line?

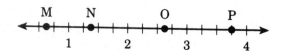

F M

G N

H O

J P

7 What number completes the number sentence shown below?

$$8 \times \square = 40 \times 60$$

A 50

B 40

C 300

D 500

GO

8 Which of these is another way to write 300 + 0.01 + 0.007 ?

   F 301.007

   G 300.017

   H 317

   J 300.17

9 Which of these is <u>not</u> equal in value to the others?

   A $\frac{6}{100}$

   B 6%

   C 0.006

   D $100\overline{)6}$

10 Which of these percentages gives the best estimate for the amount of the circle that is shaded?

   F 25%

   G 15%

   H 20%

   J 30%

11 The newspaper said that about 1300 cars cross a bridge each day. Today, the actual number of cars that crossed the bridge was 1260. To what place value was the actual number rounded to get 1300?

   A to the hundreds place

   B to the tens place

   C to the thousands place

   D to the ones place

12 In the numeral 274,958, the 4 means —

   F 40 thousand

   G 4 hundred

   H 4 hundred thousands

   J 4 thousand

13 Which of these is between 0.045 and 0.07?

   A 0.052

   B 0.042

   C 0.083

   D 0.029

14 Which of these is a composite number?

   F 7

   G 5

   H 91

   J 29

15
$$\begin{array}{r} -9 \\ +6 \\ \hline \end{array}$$

   A +3

   B −3

   C +15

   D −15

16 What is the smallest number that can be divided evenly by 7 and 28?

   F 14

   G 112

   H 56

   J 36

ANSWER ROWS   **8** Ⓕ Ⓖ Ⓗ Ⓙ   **11** Ⓐ Ⓑ Ⓒ Ⓓ   **14** Ⓕ Ⓖ Ⓗ Ⓙ

         9 Ⓐ Ⓑ Ⓒ Ⓓ   **12** Ⓕ Ⓖ Ⓗ Ⓙ   **15** Ⓐ Ⓑ Ⓒ Ⓓ

       10 Ⓕ Ⓖ Ⓗ Ⓙ   **13** Ⓐ Ⓑ Ⓒ Ⓓ   **16** Ⓕ Ⓖ Ⓗ Ⓙ

NUMBER RIGHT _____

Lesson 5   Addition

Example

Directions: Mark the space for the correct answer to each addition problem. Choose "None of these" if the right answer is not given.

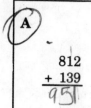

```
   812
 + 139
 ‾‾‾‾‾
   951
```

A 1051
B   942
C   852
D   941
E   None of these

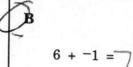

$6 + {}^-1 = 7$

F −8
G   5
H   7
J −5
K   None of these

Tips

If the answer you find is not one of the answer choices, rework the problem on scratch paper.

If you rework a problem and still find that the right answer is not given, mark the space for "None of these."

Practice

1
```
   4982
      9
    274
 + 5613
 ‾‾‾‾‾‾
  10,878
```

A 10,877
B 10,878
C   9878
D   9877
E None of these

2

$12 + {}^-8 =$

F   20
G −4
H −20
J   4
K None of these

3

$\frac{1}{4} + \frac{2}{3} + \frac{3}{8} =$

A $1\frac{5}{24}$
B $\frac{6}{15}$
C $1\frac{7}{24}$
D $\frac{6}{24}$
E None of these

4

$\frac{21}{100} + \frac{7}{10} =$

F 0.91
G 0.28
H 1.48
J 0.721
K None of these

5

$0.723 + 0.028 =$

A 0.931
B 0.7258
C 0.951
D 0.741
E None of these

6

$65.37 + 0.882 =$

F   66.252
G 650.252
H   65.919
J 605.919
K None of these

7

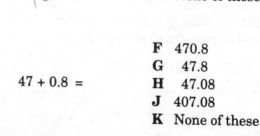

```
   866
 +  59
 ‾‾‾‾‾
   925
```

A 813
B 825
C 925
D 815
E None of these

8

$47 + 0.8 =$

F 470.8
G   47.8
H   47.08
J 407.08
K None of these

112

GO

9

$5\frac{1}{8}$
$+\ 2\frac{2}{5}$

A $3\frac{1}{5}$
B 8
C $7\frac{21}{40}$
D $8\frac{3}{13}$
E None of these

10

5.627
$+\ .228$
$\overline{5.855}$

F 5.201
G 5.855
H 5.845
J 5.835
K None of these

11

$\frac{1}{2} + \frac{4}{5} =$

A $\frac{9}{10}$
B 1
C $1\frac{1}{5}$
D $\frac{5}{7}$
E None of these

12

$4592.88 + 5.5 =$

F 4598.38
G 45,925.38
H 45,926.38
J 4597.38
K None of these

13 $18.6 + 0.072 + 4.79 =$

A 22.462
B 22.672
C 23.751
D 23.462
E None of these

14

$825.916 + 23.57 =$

F 849.586
G 850.486
H 849.486
J 84.9486
K None of these

15

$9\frac{5}{9}$
$+\ \frac{5}{6}$

A $9\frac{1}{3}$
B $9\frac{10}{36}$
C $10\frac{7}{9}$
D $10\frac{7}{18}$
E None of these

16

.92
.76
$+\ .21$
$\overline{1.89}$

F 10.89
G 1.89
H 18.9
J 189
K None of these

17

$5\frac{4}{10} + 3\frac{5}{10} = \square$

A $8\frac{9}{10}$
B $8\frac{9}{20}$
C $9\frac{1}{10}$
D 9
E None of these

18 $6 + {}^-9 + {}^-3 =$

F $^-6$
G 18
H 0
J 6
K None of these

STOP

Lesson 6 Subtraction

Example

Directions: Mark the space for the correct answer to each subtraction problem. Choose "NG" if the right answer is not given.

A

$4 - {}^-2 = \square$

- A 2
- B 8
- C 6
- D -2
- E NG

B

105
− 0.5

- F 100
- G 105.5
- H 103.5
- J 65
- K NG

Tips

If the right answer is not given, mark the space for "NG." This means "not given."

When you are not sure of an answer, check it by adding.

Practice

1

559
− 89

- A 570
- B 539
- C 439
- D 470
- E NG

2

$36.8 - 4.1 =$

- F 31.13
- G 32.79
- H 32.7
- J 40.9
- K NG

3

$40 - .64 = \square$

- A 39.46
- B 40.64
- C 40.36
- D 24
- E NG

4

4175
− 2856

- F 1319
- G 2721
- H 2319
- J 7031
- K NG

5

54.6
− 0.87

- A 54.27
- B 53.73
- C 53.63
- D 54.73
- E NG

6

$6 - {}^-8 =$

- F 2
- G -2
- H -14
- J 14
- K NG

7

$20.01 - 0.09 =$

- A 19.92
- B 19.11
- C 20.01
- D 20.11
- E NG

8

9.847
− 4.216

- F 4.631
- G 5.631
- H 5.629
- J 4.629
- K NG

GO

9

$8\frac{7}{8}$
$-\ 1\frac{1}{4}$

   A $7\frac{1}{7}$
   B 10
   C $8\frac{5}{8}$
   D 11
   E NG

10

$\frac{10}{19} - \frac{6}{19} = \square$

   F 4
   G $\frac{4}{19}$
   H $\frac{14}{19}$
   J $\frac{1}{3}$
   K NG

11

$\frac{7}{13}$
$-\ \frac{4}{13}$

   A $\frac{11}{13}$
   B $\frac{3}{26}$
   C $\frac{3}{13}$
   D $\frac{11}{26}$
   E NG

12

$6\frac{1}{4} - \frac{3}{4} =$

   F $5\frac{1}{2}$
   G $6\frac{1}{4}$
   H $6\frac{1}{2}$
   J $5\frac{3}{4}$
   K NG

13

$7.3 - 0.3 =$

   A 6.27
   B 3.3
   C 4.3
   D 7
   E NG

14

$-4 - 8 =$

   F 12
   G −12
   H 4
   J −4
   K NG

15

47.46
$-\ \ 0.57$

   A 47.12
   B 46.98
   C 46.89
   D 47.99
   E NG

16

$4867.2 - 12 =$

   F 4866
   G 4867.18
   H 4867.12
   J 4855.2
   K NG

17

$23.045 - .274 =$

   A 23.231
   B 22.671
   C 22.679
   D 23.771
   E NG

18

762
$-\ \ 0.052$

   F 761.948
   G 761.48
   H 762.958
   J 761.958
   K NG

19

$-18 - 5 =$

   A 13
   B −13
   C 23
   D −23
   E NG

STOP

Example

Directions: Mark the space for the correct answer to each multiplication problem. Choose "NH" if the right answer is not given.

A

3.6
x .2

A 72
B 7.2
C 0.72
D 6.2
E NH

B

$^-2 \times 14 =$

F 29
G −29
H 16
J −16
K NH

If the right answer is not given, mark the space for "NH." This means "not here."

Take your best guess when you are unsure of the answer. If you can eliminate answer choices before guessing, you will improve your chances of choosing the correct answer.

Practice

1

6.01
x 7.92

A 47.5992
B 13.93
C 42.92
D 47.4992
E NH

2

$(2 + 4)3^2 =$

F 26
G 18
H 38
J 54
K NH

3

0.2
x 0.9

A 0.11
B 11
C 0.19
D 19
E NH

4

10% of □ = 15

F 0.15
G 150
H 15
J 1.5
K NH

5

$8 \times \frac{7}{8} =$

A $8\frac{1}{8}$
B $\frac{56}{8}$
C 7
D $\frac{7}{64}$
E NH

6

498
x 22

F 10,956
G 10,222
H 9956
J 9922
K NH

7

330 x .01 =

A 33
B 3.03
C 0.303
D 3.3
E NH

8

20,409
x 6001

F 12,474,409
G 122,474,409
H 122,474,009
J 12,475,409
K NH

116

GO

ANSWER ROWS   A Ⓐ Ⓑ Ⓒ Ⓓ Ⓔ   1 Ⓐ Ⓑ Ⓒ Ⓓ Ⓔ   3 Ⓐ Ⓑ Ⓒ Ⓓ Ⓔ   5 Ⓐ Ⓑ Ⓒ Ⓓ Ⓔ   7 Ⓐ Ⓑ Ⓒ Ⓓ Ⓔ
          B Ⓕ Ⓖ Ⓗ Ⓙ Ⓚ   2 Ⓕ Ⓖ Ⓗ Ⓙ Ⓚ   4 Ⓕ Ⓖ Ⓗ Ⓙ Ⓚ   6 Ⓕ Ⓖ Ⓗ Ⓙ Ⓚ   8 Ⓕ Ⓖ Ⓗ Ⓙ Ⓚ

9

$5\frac{2}{3}$ x 9 =

A $45\frac{2}{3}$

B $\frac{18}{27}$

C 51

D $48\frac{1}{3}$

E NG

10

$\frac{5}{12}$ x $\frac{3}{8}$ =

F $5\frac{1}{96}$

G 8

H $\frac{15}{91}$

J $\frac{5}{32}$

K NG

11

16 x $\frac{3}{4}$ =

A 12

B $4\frac{1}{4}$

C $\frac{3}{64}$

D $12\frac{1}{4}$

E NG

12

$\frac{4}{9}$ x $\frac{1}{2}$ =

F $\frac{5}{18}$

G $\frac{2}{9}$

H $9\frac{1}{2}$

J $\frac{2}{18}$

K NG

13

13 + 2 x 4 =

A 20

B 60

C 19

D 64

E NG

PEMDAS

13 + 8 = 21

14

5 x ⁻8 x 2 =

F 80

G 50

H ⁻50

J ⁻80

K NG

15

.402
x .705

A 28.3401

B 0.28341

C 2.831

D 28.341

E NG

16

10% of 18 =

F 108

G 0.108

H 1.8

J 0.18

K NG

17

0.41 x 0.15 =

A 0.0615

B 41.15

C 0.415

D 61.5

E NG

18

3085
x 206

F 635,501

G 635,410

H 605,510

J 63,551

K NG

19 24 is what percent of 96?

A 36%

B 30%

C 24%

D 25%

E NG

ANSWER ROWS
9 Ⓐ Ⓑ Ⓒ Ⓓ Ⓔ   12 Ⓕ Ⓖ Ⓗ Ⓙ Ⓚ   15 Ⓐ Ⓑ Ⓒ Ⓓ Ⓔ   18 Ⓕ Ⓖ Ⓗ Ⓙ Ⓚ
10 Ⓕ Ⓖ Ⓗ Ⓙ Ⓚ   13 Ⓐ Ⓑ Ⓒ Ⓓ Ⓔ   16 Ⓕ Ⓖ Ⓗ Ⓙ Ⓚ   19 Ⓐ Ⓑ Ⓒ Ⓓ Ⓔ
11 Ⓐ Ⓑ Ⓒ Ⓓ Ⓔ   14 Ⓕ Ⓖ Ⓗ Ⓙ Ⓚ   17 Ⓐ Ⓑ Ⓒ Ⓓ Ⓔ

117

Example

Directions: Mark the space for the correct answer to each division problem. Choose "N" if the right answer is not given.

A $4\overline{)38}$	A 8 B 8.5 C 9 D N	B $\frac{1}{8} \div \frac{1}{2} =$	F $\frac{1}{4}$ G $1\frac{1}{4}$ H $\frac{1}{16}$ J N

Pay close attention when you are dividing decimals or fractions. It is easy to make a mistake by misplacing the decimal point or forgetting to invert fractions.

If the right answer is not given, mark the space for "N." This means the answer is not given.

Practice

1 $^-54 \div 6 =$
A 48
B -9
C 9
D N

2 $7\overline{)1.435}$
F 2.05
G 2.5
H 0.205
J N

3 $\frac{1}{7} \div \frac{5}{7} =$
A $\frac{1}{5}$
B $1\frac{2}{7}$
C $\frac{5}{49}$
D N

4 $4.29 \div 10 =$
F 0.0429
G 10.429
H 42.9
J N

5 $84 \div 12 = \square$
A 8
B 7
C 8 R4
D N

6 $40\overline{)2497}$
F 63
G 63 R4
H 62 R17
J N

7 $.35\overline{).105}$
A 30
B 0.3
C 0.035
D N

8 $225\overline{)189}$
F 0.84
G 84
H 8.04
J N

GO

ANSWER ROWS
A Ⓐ Ⓑ Ⓒ Ⓓ
B Ⓕ Ⓖ Ⓗ Ⓙ
1 Ⓐ Ⓑ Ⓒ Ⓓ
2 Ⓕ Ⓖ Ⓗ Ⓙ
3 Ⓐ Ⓑ Ⓒ Ⓓ
4 Ⓕ Ⓖ Ⓗ Ⓙ
5 Ⓐ Ⓑ Ⓒ Ⓓ
6 Ⓕ Ⓖ Ⓗ Ⓙ
7 Ⓐ Ⓑ Ⓒ Ⓓ
8 Ⓕ Ⓖ Ⓗ Ⓙ

Lesson 8   Division

(9)

$347 \div 100 =$

347
+ 100
———
449

A   3.47
B   103.47
C   34.7
(D)   N

10

$6\overline{)7818}$

F   133
G   1298
H   1303
J   N

11

$54 \div 2\frac{1}{4} =$

A $27\frac{1}{4}$
B   24
C $24\frac{1}{4}$
D   N

12

$4\frac{1}{8} \div 3\frac{2}{3} =$

F $\frac{8}{9}$
G $1\frac{1}{8}$
H $1\frac{1}{3}$
J   N

13

$\frac{19 + (48 \div 6)}{3} =$

A   43
B   27
C   9
D   N

14

$\frac{5}{14} \div \frac{2}{7} =$

F $1\frac{1}{4}$
G $2\frac{1}{7}$
H $\frac{10}{98}$
J   N

15

$^-63 \div {}^-9 =$

A   -7
B   -9
C   6
D   N

16

$40.8 \div 0.6 =$

F   68
G   240.8
H   680
J   N

17

$\frac{^-56}{^-14} =$

A   -6
B   16
C   4
D   N

18

$0.002 \div 500 =$

F   40
G   0.4
H   4
J   N

19

$167.238 \div 6.52 =$

A   26.65
B   275.65
C   25.65
D   N

20   Estimate the answer for this item.

$9357 \div 216\frac{9}{10}$

is closest to

F   500
G   50
H   4000
J   N

STOP

ANSWER ROWS

9 Ⓐ Ⓑ Ⓒ Ⓓ   12 Ⓕ Ⓖ Ⓗ Ⓙ   15 Ⓐ Ⓑ Ⓒ Ⓓ   18 Ⓕ Ⓖ Ⓗ Ⓙ
10 Ⓕ Ⓖ Ⓗ Ⓙ   13 Ⓐ Ⓑ Ⓒ Ⓓ   16 Ⓕ Ⓖ Ⓗ Ⓙ   19 Ⓐ Ⓑ Ⓒ Ⓓ
11 Ⓐ Ⓑ Ⓒ Ⓓ   14 Ⓕ Ⓖ Ⓗ Ⓙ   17 Ⓐ Ⓑ Ⓒ Ⓓ   20 Ⓕ Ⓖ Ⓗ Ⓙ

119

Example   **Directions:** Mark the space for the correct answer to each problem. Choose "None of these" if the correct answer is not given.

E1

$200 \overline{)300}$

A 1500
B   150
C   67
D   230
E None of these

E2

$0.8 \div .25 =$

F   3.2
G 20
H   0.2
J   0.55
K None of these

1

$956.4 - 83.88 =$

A 873.48
B 873.52
C 872.53
D 872.52
E None of these

(handwritten work)
956.14
83.88
870.68

6

$4 + {}^-8 + {}^-6 =$

F   18
G −18
H   10
J   −2
K None of these

2

28
49
70
+ 53

F 200
G 210
H 190
J 180
K None of these

7

$0.7 \overline{)5.964}$

A   0.82
B   8.52
C 52.57
D   0.0852
E None of these

3

816
x 495

A 393,920
B   32,392
C   40,392
D 403,930
E None of these

(handwritten) $403,920$

8

$2 \times {}^-6 \times 3 =$

F −36
G 416
H   18
J   56
K None of these

4

$24 \times 0.672 =$

F   24.672
G   16.128
H 162.8
J 161.28
K None of these

9

25007
− 8469

A 16,532
B 17,462
C 17,538
D 16,538
E None of these

5

$\frac{3}{5} \div 12 =$

A 20
B $2\frac{1}{5}$
C $2\frac{1}{12}$
D $\frac{1}{20}$
E None of these

10 $(15 - 6)(4 + 5) =$

F   81
G 150
H   41
J 189
K None of these

GO

PEMDAS

11

$\frac{1}{4}$
$\frac{1}{18}$
$+ \frac{1}{3}$

A $\frac{23}{36}$

B 1

C $1\frac{1}{6}$

D $\frac{2}{3}$

E None of these

12

5 is what % of 40?

F 25

G 12.5

H 10

J 30.5

K None of these

13

90 − ⁻30 =

A 3

B −30

C −60

D 30

E None of these

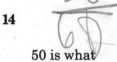

14

50 is what
percent of 2000?

F 25%

G 30%

H 300%

J 2.5%

K None of these

15

5.39 − .6 =

A 5.33

B 4.79

C 4.69

D 0.61

E None of these

16

$\frac{(25 - 9) + 20}{4}$

F 21

G 11

H 9

J 24

K None of these

17

$4^2 \div (2 + 6) =$

A 0.5

B 1

C 8

D 4

E None of these

18

$(60 + 24) \div 12 =$

F 62

G 7

H 29

J 8

K None of these

19

36.85
x   20

A 720.85

B 7370

C 56.85

D 737

E None of these

20

150 ÷ ⁻30 =

F −5

G 50

H 120

J −20

K None of these

21

$18\frac{4}{15}$
$- 10\frac{3}{5}$

A $6\frac{3}{4}$

B $5\frac{3}{8}$

C 6

D $7\frac{2}{3}$

E None of these

22

$\frac{2}{3}$ x 27 =

F 16

G 9

H 18

J 6

K None of these

STOP

Example   **Directions:** Find the correct answer to each geometry problem. Mark the space for your choice.

A The triangle on the right has two angles that measure 90° and 50°. What is the measure of the third angle?

  A 220°

  B 50°

  C 30°

  D 40°

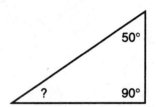

 Read the question carefully and think about what you are supposed to do. Then look for key words, numbers, and figures before you choose an answer.

Practice

1 The map below shows the distances between six cities in Central County. Suppose you wanted to go from City 4 to City 1. What is the shortest distance you must travel?

Central County

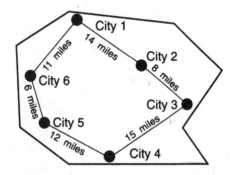

  A 37 miles

  B 27 miles

  C 17 miles

  D 29 miles

2 What is the volume of a freezer that is 6 feet high, 4 feet wide, and 3 feet deep?

  F 72 cu ft

  G 27 cu ft

  H 13 cu ft

  J 62 cu ft

3 Which number sentence shows how to find the area of a lawn that is 12 yd by 18 yd?

  A Area = (2 x 12 yd) + (2 x 18 yd)

  B Area = 12 yd + 18 yd

  C Area = 12 yd x 18 yd

  D 90 square meters

4 Which of these is an obtuse angle?

  F 90°

  G 120°

  H 12°

  J 0°

GO

ANSWER ROWS   **A** Ⓐ Ⓑ Ⓒ Ⓓ   **1** Ⓐ Ⓑ Ⓒ Ⓓ   **2** Ⓕ Ⓖ Ⓗ Ⓙ   **3** Ⓐ Ⓑ Ⓒ Ⓓ   **4** Ⓕ Ⓖ Ⓗ Ⓙ

5 The two cubes below are identical in size. What shape would be formed if you joined the cubes together end to end?

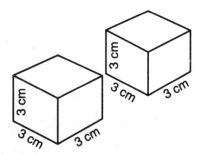

A a rectangular prism with dimensions 3 cm by 3 cm by 9 cm

B a cube with dimensions 6 cm by 6 cm by 6 cm

C a rectangular prism with dimensions 3 cm by 3 cm by 6 cm

D a cube with dimensions 9 cm by 9 cm by 9 cm

6 In the picture below, Figure A and Figure B are congruent. What is the perimeter of Figure A?

Figure A   Figure B

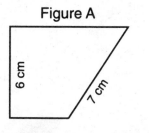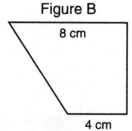

F 25 cm

G 13 cm

H 42 cm

J It can't be found.

7 Which of these statements is true?

A A right angle is 100°.

B Perpendicular lines never intersect.

C Parallel lines form a 90° angle.

D Two rays make up an angle.

8 What is the best estimate of the measure of angle FLJ in the figure below?

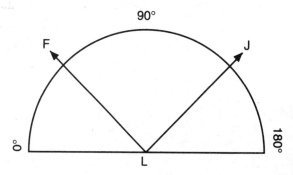

F 45°

G 90°

H 135°

J 180°

9 In the figure below, all the angles are right angles. What is the area of the figure?

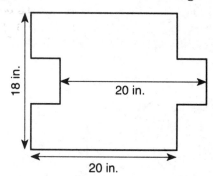

A 58 sq. in.

B 360 sq. in.

C 7200 sq. in.

D 340 sq. in.

10 In triangle ABC, just two of the angles are equal. What kind of triangle is it?

F a right triangle

G an equilateral triangle

H an isosceles triangle

J a parallel triangle

123

GO

11 What is the volume of the rectangular prism shown below?

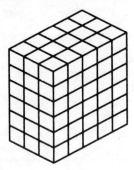

 = 1 unit of volume

A 14 units

B 60 units

C 63 units

D 90 units

12 The radius of the circle below is —

F the same as $\overline{PN}$

G half of $\overline{OM}$

H half of $\overline{MN}$

J the same as $\overline{ON}$

13 What is the area of a piece of cardboard that is 15 inches long and 12 inches wide?

A 180 square inches

B 27 square inches

C 54 square inches

D 270 square inches

14 A family is building a fence in their yard. The fence will be the same shape as the yard, but will be 1 foot inside each edge of the yard. How long will the fence be?

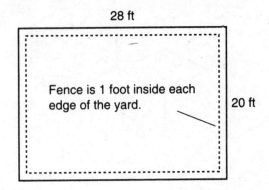

F 96 ft

G 88 ft

H 92 ft

J 95 ft

15 Look at Shape A. Suppose you rotated the shape one-half turn clockwise. What would the shape look like?

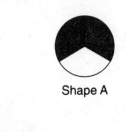

Shape A

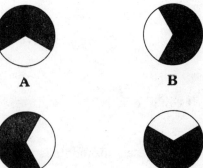

A   B

C   D

124

GO

ANSWER ROWS   **11** Ⓐ Ⓑ Ⓒ Ⓓ   **13** Ⓐ Ⓑ Ⓒ Ⓓ   **15** Ⓐ Ⓑ Ⓒ Ⓓ

12 Ⓕ Ⓖ Ⓗ Ⓙ   **14** Ⓕ Ⓖ Ⓗ Ⓙ

16 How many of the shaded shapes will it take to cover the grid shown below?

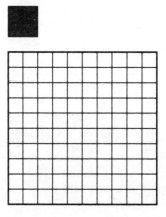

F 100

G 40

H 25

J 20

17 Molly and Rudy both have square yards. The sides of Rudy's yard are half as long as the sides of Molly's yard. Which of these statements is true about their yards?

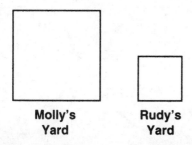

Molly's Yard   Rudy's Yard

A The area of Rudy's yard is $\frac{1}{2}$ the area of Molly's yard.

B The area of Rudy's yard is $\frac{1}{4}$ the area of Molly's yard.

C The area of Rudy's yard is $\frac{1}{8}$ the area of Molly's yard.

D The area of Rudy's yard is $\frac{3}{4}$ the area of Molly's yard.

18 Look at this rectangular prism. Which plane is parallel to ADCB?

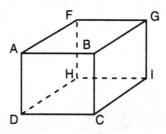

F FHIG

G ABFG

H DHIC

J AHIB

19 The two figures below are similar. What is the perimeter of the smaller figure?

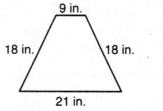

A 66 in.

B 33 in.

C 28 in.

D 22 in.

20 Which of these statements would prove that the triangle below is equilateral?

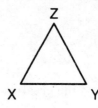

F XY = XZ + YZ

G Angle YXZ = 90°

H Angle YZX = 60°

J XY = (XZ + YZ) ÷ 3

STOP

Example   **Directions:** Find the correct answer to each measurement problem. Mark the space for your choice.

A About how many centimeters long is $\overline{XZ}$?

   A 4 centimeters

   B 8 centimeters

   C 5 centimeters

   D 10 centimeters

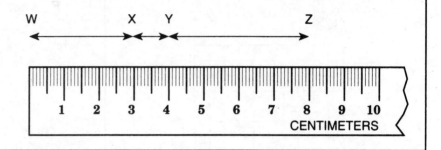

If you are confused by a problem, read it again. If you are still confused, skip the problem and come back to it later.

For some problems, you will have to work on scratch paper. Be sure to transfer numbers accurately and compute carefully.

Practice

1 Suppose you had 10 coins in your pocket totaling $.54. Which of the following statements is true about the coins?

   A Some of the coins are nickels.

   B None of the coins are pennies.

   C Two of the coins are quarters.

   D Five of the coins are dimes.

2 A bottle holds 4 liters of water. If you drink 1500 milliliters of water, how much will be left in the jar? (1 liter = 1000 milliliters)

   F 3500 milliliters

   G 5500 milliliters

   H 2500 milliliters

   J 4850 milliliters

3 Which of these is the greatest volume?

   A 18 pints

   B 12 quarts

   C 2 gallons

   D 30 cups

4 Charlie flew from Texas to California. When he arrived, he called his friend Maxine in New York. Charlie made the call at 8:00 P.M. California time. In New York, it was 3 hours later. What time was it in New York when Maxine received the call?

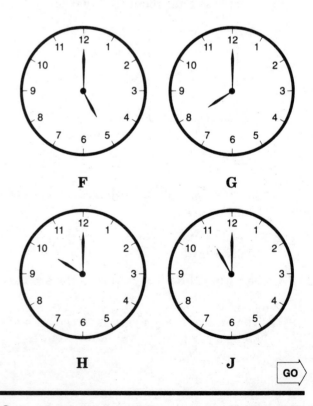

GO

5 A bus was scheduled to leave the station at 2:25 P.M. Because of a rain storm, the bus was delayed for 2 hours and 50 minutes. What time did the bus leave the station?

A 4:15 P.M.

B 4:25 P.M.

C 5:15 P.M.

D 5:25 P.M.

6 A worker had a roll of tape that was 12 yards long. She cut 5 feet of tape from the roll. How much tape was left on the roll?

F 10 yards

G 7 yards

H 9 yards and 2 feet

J 10 yards and 1 foot

7 How many inches are in 8 feet?

A 96

B 80

C 84

D 98

8 An unsharpened pencil is about how long?

F 16 inches

G 1 foot

H 1 inch

J 6 inches

9 The Harmon family heats their house with a coal burning stove. When the coal is delivered by truck, the weight of the coal is probably given in —

A pounds

B tons

C ounces

D gallons

10 Which of these might be 4 yards wide by 8 yards long?

F a small closet in a bedroom

G a kitchen table

H a one-car garage

J a bed

11 The height of a mountain would probably be given in —

A meters

B miles

C inches

D centimeters

12 What fraction of a yard is 30 inches?

F $\frac{5}{2}$

G $\frac{5}{6}$

H $\frac{3}{4}$

J $\frac{3}{10}$

13 The scale on the drawing of a house shows that 2 centimeters = 1 meter. What would the real dimensions of the living room be if it was 8 centimeters by 12 centimeters on the drawing?

A 8 meters by 12 meters

B 16 meters by 24 meters

C 6 meters by 10 meters

D 4 meters by 6 meters

14 3967 millimeters is equal to —

F 0.03967 meters

G 39.67 meters

H 3.967 meters

J 3000.967 meters

STOP

Lesson 12   Problem Solving

Example   **Directions:** Find the correct answer to each problem. Mark the space for your choice.

A A lake is normally 24 feet deep. Which number sentence shows the depth after a storm makes the lake 2 feet deeper?

    A 24 - 2 =☐

    B 24 + 2 =☐

    C 24 x 2 =☐

    D 24 ÷ 2 =☐

B Sandra bought 20 baskets for $2.00 each and sold them for $5.00 each. How much did she make all together?

    F $100

    G $40

    H $23

    J Not Given

Choose "Not Given" only if you are sure the right answer is not one of the choices.

Read each problem carefully. Look for key words, numbers, and figures in each problem. If you must work on scratch paper, be sure you perform the correct operation.

Practice

1 There are 25 students in a class. Sixty percent of them are girls. Each girl volunteers 45 minutes a week in the library. Which number sentence shows how much time they volunteer all together in 4 weeks?

    A [(25 x 60) x 45] x 4 =☐

    B (25 x .6) + (45 x 4) = ☐

    C [(25 x .6) + 45] x 4 =☐

    D [(25 x .6) x 45] x 4 =☐

2 The bus ride from Alonzo's house to school is 7 miles. The ride home is only 4 miles because the driver uses a different route. Alonzo rides the bus 5 days each week and goes to school for 38 weeks each year. Which of these shows how far Alonzo travels by school bus each year?

    F (7 + 4) x (5 + 38) =☐

    G (7 + 4) x (5 x 38) =☐

    H (7 x 4) x (5 x 38) =☐

    J (7 x 4) + (5 x 38) =☐

3 Regular gasoline costs $1.39 a gallon and high performance gasoline costs $1.59 a gallon. Molly's car gets 30 miles per gallon of gas and her gas tank holds 15 gallons. Which of these questions can <u>not</u> be answered using only the information given?

    A How much will it cost Molly to drive back and forth to the mall?

    B How much will it cost Molly to fill up her gas tank?

    C How far can Molly drive if her tank is filled?

    D How much does it cost Molly to drive one mile using regular gas?

4 Skis normally sell for $300. They are on sale for $270. What percentage discount is this off the regular price?

    F 30%

    G 10%

    H 27%

    J 11.1%

GO

ANSWER ROWS   A Ⓐ Ⓑ Ⓒ Ⓓ   1 Ⓐ Ⓑ Ⓒ Ⓓ   3 Ⓐ Ⓑ Ⓒ Ⓓ

128   B Ⓕ Ⓖ Ⓗ Ⓙ   2 Ⓕ Ⓖ Ⓗ Ⓙ   4 Ⓕ Ⓖ Ⓗ Ⓙ

The graph below shows the prices of five different cars. Use the graph to answer questions 5, 6, and 7.

Prices of Five Cars

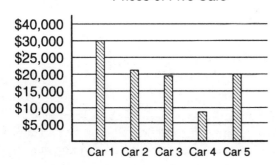

5 Which of these is closest to the average price of the five cars?

   A $15,000

   B $17,000

   C $23,000

   D $20,000

6 Car 1 is on sale for 15% off the regular price. How much would the car cost if you bought it on sale?

   F $15,000

   G $25,500

   H $28,500

   J Not Given

7 Nadine wants to buy Car 5. She already owns a car, and the dealer will pay her $3000 for it. In the state where Nadine lives, there is a 5% sales tax. What is the total price Nadine must pay for her car?

   A $17,850

   B $18,000

   C $17,000

   D $21,000

8 Donna, Len, and their friends are spending Saturday downtown shopping, going to the movies, and having dinner. They got on the subway at 9:15 and arrived at City Hall station at 10:05. How long did the subway ride take?

   F 60 minutes

   G 1 hour and 5 minutes

   H 55 minutes

   J Not Given

9 Donna and Len had $35 to spend on gifts for their parents. They had earned the money recycling aluminum cans. Donna earned $5 more than Len. How much did Len earn?

   A $20.00

   B $30.00

   C $15.00

   D $10.00

10 At lunch, Donna ordered a sandwich and soft drink for $3.50 and Len ordered pizza and milk for $4.50. Their friends ordered meals that totaled $22.00. The group decided to give the waiter a tip of 15%. What was the total cost of the meal, including the tip?

   F $31.50

   G $34.50

   H $45.00

   J Not Given

11 The mall in the Plaza Building has 56 stores. Donna and Len shopped in $\frac{2}{7}$ of them. In how many stores did they shop?

   A 8

   B 28

   C 16

   D 18

GO

The chart below shows the nightly rates at a campground. Use the chart to answer questions 12 through 14.

CAMPGROUND RATES		
	10' x 20'	20' x 40'
Without Electricity	$7.00	$10.00
With Electricity	$9.00	$12.00
From September to May, rates are reduced by $3.00 per night.		

12 How much would it cost to stay 5 nights at a 10' x 20' camp site without electricity?

F $50.00

G $36.00

H $45.00

J   Not Given

13 When the Armenta family went camping, they planned to stay 10 nights at a small site without electricity. After 2 nights, they moved to a large site with electricity. They stayed at this site for the rest of their vacation. How much did they spend in all for their stay at the campground?

A $110.00

B $100.00

C $64.00

D $86.00

14 What percentage would you save on the cost of a large camp site with electricity if you stayed at the campground in October rather than in July?

F   30%

G   33%

H   25%

J   Not Given

15 The Carbondale School has 685 students and 32 teachers. One day, 134 students and 5 teachers were absent because of the flu. How many students and teachers in all were present at school that day?

A   583

B   578

C   139

D   Not Given

16 A softball player gets a hit 4 out of every 15 times she comes to bat. She batted 45 times last season. How many hits did she get?

F   34

G   7

H   11

J   Not Given

17 A carpenter is building a door for a closet. The opening of the closet is 7 feet tall and 30 inches wide. The wood the carpenter will use is 8 inches wide. What other information does he need to determine how many pieces of wood to buy?

A   the cost of the pieces of wood

B   the thickness of the pieces of wood

C   the length of the pieces of wood

D   the diagonal dimension of the opening

18 Tony and Deena are inventing a board game. They want to use a six-side block with one of the vowels (A, E, I, O, and U) on each face. The letter A will be used twice. If they roll the block 30 times, how many times will the letter E probably come up?

F   5 times

G   6 times

H   10 times

J   Not Given

GO

The graph below shows the number of acres farmed in two different counties over a four-year period. Use the graph to answer questions 19 through 21.

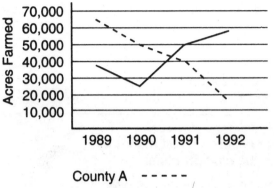

County A - - - - -

County B ————

19 Which of these might describe what is happening in County A as shown by the information on the graph?

A Houses are being torn down so the land can be used for farming.

B Farm land is being sold so it can be used to build houses.

C The price of farm land is decreasing.

D The cost of houses is decreasing.

20 In 1990, the amount of land used for farming in County B was half of what it was in 1960. About how many acres of County B were used for farming in 1960?

F 50,000 acres

G 12,500 acres

H 60,000 acres

J 25,000 acres

21 From 1989 to 1990, the amount of land farmed in County A decreased by —

A about 75%

B exactly 20%

C more than 30%

D about 25%

Read this passage and look at the chart. Then do numbers 22 through 24.

Roberto is the editor of the school paper. There are 800 students in the school. The paper is 4 pages long, and he wants to print 1000 copies.

PRINTING RATES			
	2 pages	4 pages	8 pages
250 copies	$50.00	$100.00	$160.00
500 copies	$80.00	$140.00	$260.00

22 According to the chart, how much will it probably cost to print the school paper?

F $140.00

G $280.00

H $260.00

J $400.00

23 The price per page can be found by calculating the total number of pages printed and dividing it into the cost of printing. What is the lowest price per page shown on the chart?

A 6.5 cents per page

B 2.6 cents per page

C 7 cents per page

D 10 cents per page

24 The extra copies Roberto is printing are for parents, teachers, and students' friends. If the school paper is published 4 times each year, about how much does it cost to print these extra copies?

F $208.00

G $224.00

H $390.00

J $600.00

STOP

Example   **Directions:** Find the correct answer to each measurement problem. Mark the space for your choice.

A What is the value of y in the number sentence $4y + 3 = 19$?

  A 4

  B 16

  C 22

  D 5

B 20 more than Z is 62. Which equation shows this problem?

  F $62 + 20 = Z$

  G $Z - 20 = 62$

  H $Z + 20 = 62$

  J $62 + Z = 20$

If you are sure you know which answer is correct, just mark the space for your answer and move on to the next problem.

Before you choose an answer, ask yourself, "Does this answer make sense?"

Practice

---

1 Which equation is represented by the line on this graph?

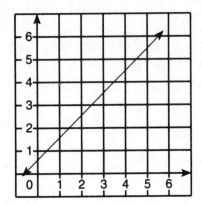

  A $y = x + 5$

  B $y = x + 0.5$

  C $y = x - 0.5$

  D $y = 0.5\,x$

2 What is a subset of the solution set for this inequality?

$$24 \div z > 3$$

  F $\{1, 2, 3, 4, 6, 8, 12\}$

  G $\{12, 36, 48\}$

  H $\{2, 3, 7, 8\}$

  J $\{2, 3, 4, 6\}$

3 $8m - 13 = 27$ $m =$

  A 5

  B 2

  C 14

  D 40

4 If $z = 9$, then $3z + 7 =$

  F 27

  G 20

  H 34

  J 4

GO

---

5 For which of these equations would $a = 5$ when $b = 9$?

A $2a + b = 19$

B $2a - b = 19$

C $b - a = 19$

D $2ab = 19$

6 What will be the coordinates of point A if you move triangle ABC three units to the right?

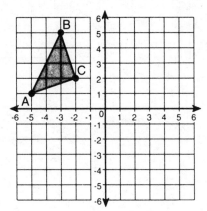

F (2, 1)

G (−2, 1)

H (3, 1)

J (−2, −1)

7 Samantha works for a construction company. Her job is to estimate the cost to build houses. One of the equations she uses is C = A x $60, where A is the area in square feet of the house and $60 is the average cost of construction per square foot. What do you think the C in the equation stands for?

A The company's estimate of the number of rooms in the house

B The cost per room of the house

C The product of the length and the width of the house

D The company's cost to build a house

8 If $5 < a$ and $a < b$, what should replace the ☐ in the expression b ☐ 5 ?

F <

G =

H >

J −

9 What number must be subtracted from 8 to get a number x that is less than $^{-}2$?

A a number greater than $^{-}2$

B a number less than 10

C a number greater than 10

D a number between $^{-}2$ and 8

10 What should replace n in the equation shown below?

$$\frac{5}{2} \times \frac{2}{n} = 1$$

F 1

G 15

H 2

J 5

11 Suppose that a and b are positive numbers and that $a < b$. What is always true about the ratio $(a \times 2) \div (b \times 2)$?

A The ratio is less than one.

B The ratio is more than one.

C The ratio is equal to one.

D The ratio is a negative number.

12 If $4y + 0 = 28$, then $y =$

F 32

G 7

H 24

J 6

STOP

ANSWER ROWS   **5** Ⓐ Ⓑ Ⓒ Ⓓ   **7** Ⓐ Ⓑ Ⓒ Ⓓ   **9** Ⓐ Ⓑ Ⓒ Ⓓ   **11** Ⓐ Ⓑ Ⓒ Ⓓ   **133**
                6 Ⓕ Ⓖ Ⓗ Ⓙ   **8** Ⓕ Ⓖ Ⓗ Ⓙ   **10** Ⓕ Ⓖ Ⓗ Ⓙ   **12** Ⓕ Ⓖ Ⓗ Ⓙ

Example   Directions: Read and work each problem. Find the correct answer. Mark the space for your choice.

E1

Gina bought 4 rolls of film. One roll can take 36 pictures. If Gina takes an average of 12 pictures a week, how long will the film last?

A (4 x 36) x 12 = ☐

B (4 ÷ 36) ÷ 12 = ☐

C (4 + 36) x 12 = ☐

D (4 x 36) ÷ 12 = ☐

E2

What is the area of a park with dimensions 48 yards by 100 yards?

F 4800 square yards

G 480 square yards

H 296 square yards

J 48,100 square yards

1 Rex studies an average of 2 hours each weekday night and 4 hours on the weekend. How long does he study each week?

A (5 x 2) + 4 = ☐

B (7 x 2) + 4 = ☐

C (5 x 4) + 2 = ☐

D 5 x (2 + 4) = ☐

2 When Caryl checked her savings account, she found she had $438.95. A week later, she withdrew $50 for the class trip. The following week, she put $65 in the bank she received for her birthday. How much money did she then have in the bank?

F $438.95 − ($50 + $65) = ☐

G $438.95 + ($50 + $65) = ☐

H $438.95 + $50 + $65 = ☐

J $438.95 − $50 + $65 = ☐

3 There are 36 inches in a yard and 1760 yards in a mile. Which of these would you use to find out how many inches were in half a mile?

A (1760 ÷ 0.5) x 36 = ☐

B (1760 x 0.5) x 36 = ☐

C 1760 x 36 = ☐ x 0.5

D (☐ x 0.5) x 36 = 1760

4 Which of these is about 150°?

F   G

H   J

5 What is the area of the *unshaded* portion of the figure below?

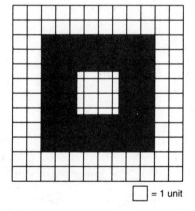

☐ = 1 unit

A 64 units

B 144 units

C 89 units

D 80 units

GO

The chart below shows the population, average income, and altitude (feet above sea level) of five different cities. Use the chart to answer numbers 6 through 8.

	Pop.	Average Income	Altitude (in feet)
Marshall	5190	$12,384	203
West Bend	10,905	$14,920	5590
Wingate	13,937	$19,375	2167
Bedford	6881	$11,934	4328
Harding	7933	$16,732	1642

6 Which of these is the approximate ratio of the average income in West Bend compared to that in Wingate?

F $\frac{5}{4}$

G $\frac{3}{4}$

H $\frac{1}{4}$

J $\frac{1}{2}$

7 If you went from Marshall to Bedford, how much would the altitude increase?

A 4125 feet

B 4531 feet

C 5387 feet

D 3125 feet

8 Which of these is the best estimate of the average population of the five towns?

F 14,000

G 6500

H 10,500

J 9000

9 What fraction of 5 pounds is 10 ounces?

A $\frac{1}{2}$

B $\frac{1}{5}$

C $\frac{1}{8}$

D $\frac{5}{16}$

10 Which of these is the greatest volume?

F 2500 milliliters

G 250 liters

H 250 milliliters

J 2.5 kiloliters

11 Which of these statements is true about points M and N?

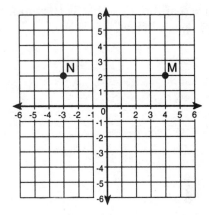

A They have the same x-coordinate.

B They have the same y-coordinate.

C They have the same x and y-coordinates.

D They both have negative x and negative y-coordinates.

12 What is the selling price of a pair of shoes if the merchant buys them for $18 and wants to sell them for 100% more?

F $35.00

G $9.00

H $118.00

J Not Given

GO

13 Louise was shipping a present to her brother. The box was 15 inches long, 12 inches wide, and 3 inches high. She taped the box using the pattern shown below so the ends of the tape don't overlap. How much tape did she use?

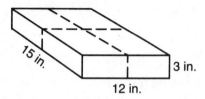

A 60 in.

B 30 in.

C 33 in.

D Not Given

14 If a = 5 and b = 4, what is the value of the expression below?

$$\frac{(4a + b)}{6} =$$

F 4

G 1.5

H 24

J Not Given

15 Doris looked at the thermometer one morning and saw it read –5°F. She knows that ice begins to melt at 32°F. Doris is going ice skating, but wants to stop before the ice begins to melt. How much must the temperature rise before Doris will have to stop skating?

A –27°F

B 27°F

C –39°F

D 37°F

16 A truck driver makes four trips a week. The distances of the trips are 1268 miles, 783 miles, 593 miles, and 1502 miles. What is the average distance he drives?

F 1136 miles

G 1136.5 miles

H 1036.5 miles

J Not Given

17 A jeweler bought 2 meters of gold chain. He used 70 centimeters for a necklace and 20 centimeters for a bracelet. How much gold chain did he have left?

A 1100 centimeters

B 1.1 meters

C 0.9 meters

D Not Given

18 What is the perimeter of the shaded shape inside the square below?

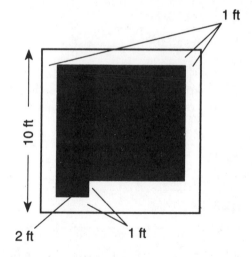

F 40 ft

G 32 ft

H 31 ft

J 36 ft

GO

19 Which statement is true about the figure shown below?

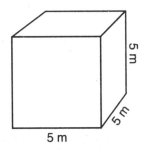

A The volume is 225 cubic meters.

B The area of each face of the cube is 15 square meters.

C The surface area is 150 square meters.

D The figure has a total of 5 faces.

20 For a school project, Ervin counted the number and kind of nuts in a can of mixed nuts. He found that there were 21 cashews, 6 Brazil nuts, 14 pecans, and 79 peanuts. If you shook the can of nuts and poured just one out, what are the odds it would be a Brazil nut?

F 6 out of 100

G 1 out of 20

H 6 out of 79

J 1 out of 60

21 How long is the rectangle shown below?

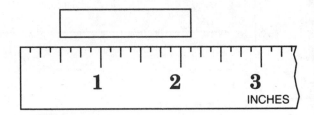

A $2\frac{1}{8}$ inches

B $2\frac{1}{2}$ inches

C $1\frac{1}{2}$ inches

D $1\frac{5}{8}$ inches

22 How much interest would you earn in 2 years on $500 in a savings account that paid 4.5% simple interest per year?

F $45.00

G $50.00

H $9.00

J $55.00

23 The Venn diagram below shows how many students in a class have a dog, a cat, or a dog and a cat. How many of the students have a cat as a pet?

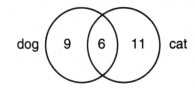

A 11

B 5

C 15

D 17

24 Four friends spent the day rock climbing. The first one to begin climbing was Carmina and the last one was Washington. Cynthia began climbing 2 minutes before Washington, and Wyatt began climbing 4 minutes after Carmina. Washington started his climb 10 minutes after Carmina. Which of these statements about the group is true?

F The order in which they began climbing was Carmina first, then Cynthia, Wyatt, and Washington.

G Wyatt began climbing eight minutes before Washington.

H Four minutes passed from when Wyatt began climbing to when Cynthia began.

J Cynthia and Wyatt began climbing at the same time.

137

STOP

ANSWER ROWS　**19** Ⓐ Ⓑ Ⓒ Ⓓ　**21** Ⓐ Ⓑ Ⓒ Ⓓ　**23** Ⓐ Ⓑ Ⓒ Ⓓ

　　　　　　　20 Ⓕ Ⓖ Ⓗ Ⓙ　**22** Ⓕ Ⓖ Ⓗ Ⓙ　**24** Ⓕ Ⓖ Ⓗ Ⓙ

NUMBER RIGHT_____

To the Student:

These tests will give you a chance to put the tips you have learned to work.

A few last reminders...

- Be sure you understand all the directions before you begin each test. You may ask the teacher questions about the directions if you do not understand them.
- Work as quickly as you can during each test.
- When you change an answer, be sure to erase your first mark completely.

- You can guess at an answer or skip difficult items and go back to them later.
- Use the tips you have learned whenever you can.
- It is OK to be a little nervous. You may even do better.

Now that you have completed the lessons in this unit, you are on your way to scoring high!

STUDENT'S NAME		SCHOOL
LAST	FIRST	MI	TEACHER

FEMALE ◯   MALE ◯

BIRTHDATE		
MONTH	DAY	YEAR

JAN ◯ FEB ◯ MAR ◯ APR ◯ MAY ◯ JUN ◯ JUL ◯ AUG ◯ SEP ◯ OCT ◯ NOV ◯ DEC ◯

GRADE ⑦ ⑧ ⑨

PART 1 CONCEPTS

E1 Ⓐ Ⓑ Ⓒ Ⓓ	4 Ⓕ Ⓖ Ⓗ Ⓙ	9 Ⓐ Ⓑ Ⓒ Ⓓ	14 Ⓕ Ⓖ Ⓗ Ⓙ	19 Ⓐ Ⓑ Ⓒ Ⓓ	24 Ⓕ Ⓖ Ⓗ Ⓙ
E2 Ⓕ Ⓖ Ⓗ Ⓙ	5 Ⓐ Ⓑ Ⓒ Ⓓ	10 Ⓕ Ⓖ Ⓗ Ⓙ	15 Ⓐ Ⓑ Ⓒ Ⓓ	20 Ⓕ Ⓖ Ⓗ Ⓙ	25 Ⓐ Ⓑ Ⓒ Ⓓ
1 Ⓐ Ⓑ Ⓒ Ⓓ	6 Ⓕ Ⓖ Ⓗ Ⓙ	11 Ⓐ Ⓑ Ⓒ Ⓓ	16 Ⓕ Ⓖ Ⓗ Ⓙ	21 Ⓐ Ⓑ Ⓒ Ⓓ	26 Ⓕ Ⓖ Ⓗ Ⓙ
2 Ⓕ Ⓖ Ⓗ Ⓙ	7 Ⓐ Ⓑ Ⓒ Ⓓ	12 Ⓕ Ⓖ Ⓗ Ⓙ	17 Ⓐ Ⓑ Ⓒ Ⓓ	22 Ⓕ Ⓖ Ⓗ Ⓙ	
3 Ⓐ Ⓑ Ⓒ Ⓓ	8 Ⓕ Ⓖ Ⓗ Ⓙ	13 Ⓐ Ⓑ Ⓒ Ⓓ	18 Ⓕ Ⓖ Ⓗ Ⓙ	23 Ⓐ Ⓑ Ⓒ Ⓓ	

PART 2 COMPUTATION

E1 Ⓐ Ⓑ Ⓒ Ⓓ Ⓔ	3 Ⓐ Ⓑ Ⓒ Ⓓ Ⓔ	7 Ⓐ Ⓑ Ⓒ Ⓓ Ⓔ	11 Ⓐ Ⓑ Ⓒ Ⓓ Ⓔ	15 Ⓐ Ⓑ Ⓒ Ⓓ Ⓔ	19 Ⓐ Ⓑ Ⓒ Ⓓ Ⓔ
E2 Ⓕ Ⓖ Ⓗ Ⓙ Ⓚ	4 Ⓕ Ⓖ Ⓗ Ⓙ Ⓚ	8 Ⓕ Ⓖ Ⓗ Ⓙ Ⓚ	12 Ⓕ Ⓖ Ⓗ Ⓙ Ⓚ	16 Ⓕ Ⓖ Ⓗ Ⓙ Ⓚ	20 Ⓕ Ⓖ Ⓗ Ⓙ Ⓚ
1 Ⓐ Ⓑ Ⓒ Ⓓ Ⓔ	5 Ⓐ Ⓑ Ⓒ Ⓓ Ⓔ	9 Ⓐ Ⓑ Ⓒ Ⓓ Ⓔ	13 Ⓐ Ⓑ Ⓒ Ⓓ Ⓔ	17 Ⓐ Ⓑ Ⓒ Ⓓ Ⓔ	21 Ⓐ Ⓑ Ⓒ Ⓓ Ⓔ
2 Ⓕ Ⓖ Ⓗ Ⓙ Ⓚ	6 Ⓕ Ⓖ Ⓗ Ⓙ Ⓚ	10 Ⓕ Ⓖ Ⓗ Ⓙ Ⓚ	14 Ⓕ Ⓖ Ⓗ Ⓙ Ⓚ	18 Ⓕ Ⓖ Ⓗ Ⓙ Ⓚ	22 Ⓕ Ⓖ Ⓗ Ⓙ Ⓚ

PART 3 APPLICATIONS

E1 Ⓐ Ⓑ Ⓒ Ⓓ	5 Ⓐ Ⓑ Ⓒ Ⓓ	11 Ⓐ Ⓑ Ⓒ Ⓓ	17 Ⓐ Ⓑ Ⓒ Ⓓ	22 Ⓕ Ⓖ Ⓗ Ⓙ	26 Ⓕ Ⓖ Ⓗ Ⓙ
E2 Ⓕ Ⓖ Ⓗ Ⓙ	6 Ⓕ Ⓖ Ⓗ Ⓙ	12 Ⓕ Ⓖ Ⓗ Ⓙ	18 Ⓕ Ⓖ Ⓗ Ⓙ	23 Ⓐ Ⓑ Ⓒ Ⓓ	27 Ⓐ Ⓑ Ⓒ Ⓓ
1 Ⓐ Ⓑ Ⓒ Ⓓ	7 Ⓐ Ⓑ Ⓒ Ⓓ	13 Ⓐ Ⓑ Ⓒ Ⓓ	19 Ⓐ Ⓑ Ⓒ Ⓓ	24 Ⓕ Ⓖ Ⓗ Ⓙ	28 Ⓕ Ⓖ Ⓗ Ⓙ
2 Ⓕ Ⓖ Ⓗ Ⓙ	8 Ⓕ Ⓖ Ⓗ Ⓙ	14 Ⓕ Ⓖ Ⓗ Ⓙ	20 Ⓕ Ⓖ Ⓗ Ⓙ	25 Ⓐ Ⓑ Ⓒ Ⓓ	29 Ⓐ Ⓑ Ⓒ Ⓓ
3 Ⓐ Ⓑ Ⓒ Ⓓ	9 Ⓐ Ⓑ Ⓒ Ⓓ	15 Ⓐ Ⓑ Ⓒ Ⓓ	21 Ⓐ Ⓑ Ⓒ Ⓓ		
4 Ⓕ Ⓖ Ⓗ Ⓙ	10 Ⓕ Ⓖ Ⓗ Ⓙ	16 Ⓕ Ⓖ Ⓗ Ⓙ			

Part 1   Concepts

Example   Directions: Read and work each problem. Find the correct answer. Mark the space for your choice.

E1

Which of these decimals is equal to $\frac{7}{8}$?

A   0.875

B   0.78

C   0.87

D   0.0875

E2

What is the smallest number that can be divided evenly by 9 and 27?

F   108

G   3

H   54

J   72

---

1 $\sqrt{121}$

A   12

B   11

C   21

D   19

2   The distance from Denver to Craig is 199 miles. From Craig to Grand junction is 153 miles. Which numbers would you use to estimate the distance from Denver to Grand Junction by going through Craig?

F   200 and 150

G   200 and 100

H   200 and 200

J   100 and 250

3   In the circle below, the shaded portion represents the percentage of students who passed a fitness test. What percentage did <u>not</u> pass the test?

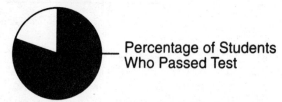

Percentage of Students Who Passed Test

A   80%

B   30%

C   10%

D   20%

4   Which of these is another way to write 9.1005?

F $(9 \times 1) + (1 \times 0.1) + (5 \times 0.01)$

G $(9 \times 0.1) + (1 \times 0.1) + (5 \times 0.0001)$

H $(9 \times 1) + (1 \times 0.1) + (5 \times 0.0001)$

J $(9 \times 1) + (1 \times 0.001) + (5 \times 0.0001)$

5   Which of these number sentences can be used to find the number that is missing from the pattern below?

$$1, 5, 13, 29, \underline{\quad}, 125$$

A $(13 + 29) = 42$

B $(29 \times 2) + 3 = 61$

C $(125 \div 5) \times 2 = 50$

D $(125 - 29) \div 2 = 48$

6   Which arrow points most closely to $-1\frac{1}{8}$?

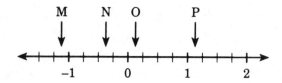

F   N

G   P

H   M

J   O

GO

7 $\frac{7}{12} = \frac{21}{\square}$

   A 26

   B 17

   C 36

   D 15

8 Which of these is 5,672,871 rounded to the nearest hundred thousand?

   F 5,600,000

   G 5,670,000

   H 5,673,000

   J 5,700,000

9 Which number sentence is <u>false</u>?

   A $^-4 > 3$

   B $^-4 > ^-13$

   C $5 > ^-2$

   D $2 > 0$

10 What number completes the number sentence below?

$$9 \times \square = 18 \times 30$$

   F 2

   G 60

   H 15

   J 3

11 How much would the value of 459,086 be decreased by replacing the 5 with a 4?

   A 10,000

   B 1000

   C 100,000

   D 100

12 What is the reciprocal of $\frac{2}{5}$?

   F $\frac{5}{2}$

   G 2.5

   H 1

   J

13 $3.91 \times 10^3 =$

   A 0.391

   B 391

   C 39,001

   D 3910

14 Which group of integers is in order from least to greatest?

   F $^-5, 3, 0, ^-2\ 3$

   G $7, ^-5, 0, 1, 8$

   H $^-3, ^-2, 0, 5, 9$

   J $3, 4, ^-7, 8, ^-9$

15 Paul went to the Post Office and found that stamps came in packages of 8 and envelopes came in packages of 6. What is the least number of each Paul can buy to have the same number of stamps and envelopes?

   A 48

   B 24

   C 18

   D 96

16 Emma stacked boxes of soap on a shelf so that there were 6 boxes in each stack. She had 3 boxes left over. Which of these could be the total number of boxes?

   F 66

   G 53

   H 39

   J 41

17 Which of these is <u>not</u> equal in value to the others?

A $\sqrt{64}$

B $\frac{48}{6}$

C $(11 - 7) \times 2$

D $1 + 3 \times 2$

18 Which of these is greater than the others?

F two and three eighths

G twenty-three hundredths

H two and eight hundredths

J two thirds

19 6^4 = *6 × 6 × 6 × 6*

A $6 + 6 + 6 + 6$

B $6 \times 6 \times 6 \times 6$

C 6×4

D $4 \times 4 \times 4 \times 4 \times 4 \times 4 \times 4$

20 Nine hundred twelve thousand, fifty =

F 91,250

G 912

H 912,050

J 901,250

21 What is the value of the expression in the box below?

$$(10 - 4)^2 \div 12$$

A 7

B 3

C 0.5

D 4

22 Which is the best estimate of $4.89 \times 23\frac{8}{9}$?

F 4×24

G 5×24

H 4×23

J 5×23

23 How would you write 43% as a fraction?

A $\frac{4}{3}$

B $\frac{3}{4}$

C $\frac{40}{30}$

D $\frac{43}{100}$

24 Which gives the prime factors of 84?

F $3 \times 2 \times 2 \times 7$

G 12×7

H $3 \times 4 \times 7$

J $3 \times 2 \times 4 + 3$

25 What should replace the ☐ in the number sentence below?

$$35 \times \square = 0.035$$

A 10^3 *= 10 × 10 × 10*

B 10^{-4}

C 10^{-3}

D 10^0

26 While reading a book about science, Veronica came upon a formula that used "the absolute value of 100." Which of these is the absolute value of 100?

F 10

G 100

H 100^2

J -100

STOP

Example   **Directions:** Find the correct answer to each problem. Mark the space for your choice. Choose "None of these" if the correct answer is not given.

E1		E2	
$-5 + 7 =$	A 3 B -3 C -2 D 12 E None of these	$\frac{2}{3} \times 27 =$	F 54 G 18 H 9 J 16 K None of these

1

$14 - {}^-3 = 11$

A 11
B -17
C -11
D 16
E None of these

6

$$278 \\ -\ \ 41$$
237

F 273
G 319
H 264
J 137
K None of these

2

$4 \times (7 + 3) =$

F 31
G 40
H 30
J 19
K None of these

7

$0.6\overline{)216}$

A 360
B 36
C 3.06
D 30.6
E None of these

3

$32.7 - 17 =$

A 32.67
B 31.3
C 15.7
D 31
E None of these

8

.33
.516
x 625
2.580
10320
309600

0.3225

F 32.35
G 0.3225
H 33.25
J 0.3335
K None of these

4

$2^3 \div (12 - 8) =$

F 5 R3
G 5.75
H 4
J 2
K None of these

9

$$\frac{9}{14} \\ -\frac{7}{14}$$

A $\frac{2}{7}$
B 2
C $\frac{1}{7}$
D $\frac{2}{9}$
E None of these

5

$\frac{5}{8} \times \frac{2}{5} =$

A $\frac{1}{4}$
B $\frac{1}{5}$
C $\frac{1}{40}$
D $\frac{1}{8}$
E None of these

10

$[51 - (15 \times 2)] \div 3 =$

F 47.5
G 41
H 10 R2
J 7
K None of these

143

GO

11

$\frac{5}{12} \div \frac{5}{6} =$

A $\frac{5}{12}$
B 2
C $\frac{1}{2}$
D $1\frac{2}{5}$
E None of these

12

65 is 20% of what number?

F 85
G 13
H 335
J 235
K None of these

13

$(20 - 11)(8 + 9) =$

A 26
B 163
C 9
D 153
E None of these

14

$\frac{-72}{-18}$

F 4
G 0.25
H −4
J 0.4
K None of these

15

$\frac{31}{40}$
$+ \frac{29}{40}$

A $1\frac{19}{40}$
B $1\frac{1}{2}$
C $2\frac{1}{10}$
D 2
E None of these

16

$4\frac{1}{5} \times \frac{4}{7} = \square$

F $4\frac{7}{20}$
G $4\frac{5}{12}$
H $7\frac{1}{2}$
J $2\frac{2}{5}$
K None of these

17

$\frac{(43 + 2) - 10}{5} =$

A 43
B 9
C 7
D −90
E None of these

18

$-23 - -8 =$

F −31
G 15
H −15
J 31
K None of these

19

$\frac{4}{100} \times \frac{3}{10} =$

A 12
B 0.12
C 0.012
D 1.2
E None of these

20

$505.7148 + 8.395 =$

F 6.24
G 62.24
H 62.2425
J 60.024
K None of these

21

$9\frac{3}{4} + 10\frac{5}{8} =$

A $21\frac{3}{4}$
B $20\frac{3}{8}$
C 20
D $19\frac{3}{8}$
E None of these

22 $18.9 + 0.037 + 4.62 =$

F 22.999
G 23.999
H 23.89
J 23.557
K None of these

STOP

Example   Directions: Read and work each problem. Find the correct answer. Mark the space for your choice.

E1

On a camping trip, 4 students shared a tent with 1 teacher. How many students and teachers were there if they needed 22 tents?

A (4 + 1) x 22 = ☐

B (4 x 1) x 22 = ☐

C (4 + 1) ÷ 22 = ☐

D (4 + 1) + 22 = ☐

E2

Joseph had 2 gallons of paint. He used 3 quarts to paint his closet. How much paint did he have left?

F 7 quarts

G 1 gallon and 2 quarts

H 5 pints

J Not Given

---

1 There are 8 windows in a house. Each window has 2 panes of glass. If it takes 3 minutes to clean one pane, how long will it take to clean all the windows?

A 3 x 2 ÷ 8 = ☐

B (3 + 2) ÷ 8 = ☐

C 3 ÷ 2 ÷ 8 = ☐

D 3 x 2 x 8 = ☐

2 Leon has $250.00 in his bank account. The account earns 4% interest a year. How much money will he have in his savings account at the end of a year?

F $250 x .04 = ☐

G $250 + ($250 x .04) = ☐

H $250 x ($250 x .04) = ☐

J $250 + $250 + .04 = ☐

3 The gas tank in a car holds 20 gallons. It is now $\frac{1}{4}$ full. If gas costs $1.25 a gallon, how much will it cost to fill the tank?

A 20 x $\frac{1}{4}$ + $1.25 = ☐

B 20 ÷ ($\frac{3}{4}$ x $1.25) = ☐

C $1.25 x (20 x $\frac{3}{4}$) = ☐

D $1.25 x $\frac{1}{4}$ x 20 = ☐

---

4 What is the median of the following set of numbers?

{3, 2, 2, 3, 2, 6}

F 2

G 6

H 3

J 4

5 What is the figure below called?

A an angle

B a line

C a ray

D a line segment

6 137 milliliters is the same as —

F 0.0137 liters

G 1.37 liters

H 0.137 liters

J 1370 liters

7 If $3x - 14 = 40$, then $x =$

A 15

B 8

C 18

D 12

GO ▷

8   In the figure below, which pair of angles is complementary?

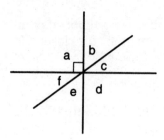

    F   a and b

    G   a and f

    H   b and d

    J   b and c

9   Suppose you had 15 coins that totaled $2.00. None of them are pennies and none are half-dollars. Which of these might you have?

    A   10 dimes and 5 quarters

    B   4 nickels, 5 dimes, and 4 quarters

    C   5 nickels, 5 dimes, and 5 quarters

    D   5 nickels, 4 dimes, and 6 quarters

10   Two out of five people who shop at a supermarket pay by check. If 175 people shop at the supermarket, how many of them pay by check?

    F   70

    G   150

    H   140

    J   35

11   What number must be added to 7 to get a number x that is less than −5 but greater than −10?

    A   a number greater than 16

    B   a number between −17 and −12

    C   a number between 0 and −9

    D   a number less than −17

The graph below shows the amount of money five students saved in two years. Use the graph to answer questions 12 through 14.

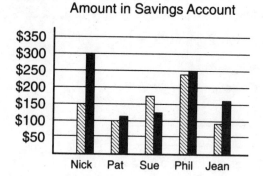

12   Which student's savings doubled from 1991 to 1992?

    F   Pat

    G   Jean

    H   Sue

    J   Not Given

13   Even though Pat didn't deposit any money in 1992, the amount of money she had in her account increased because of the interest she earned. About what rate of interest did she receive on her money?

    A   30%

    B   10%

    C   3%

    D   105%

14   Based on the graph, which student might have deposited $50 in January of 1992 and withdrawn $100 in April?

    F   Jean

    G   Nick

    H   Sue

    J   Phil

15 The two figures below are congruent. Which is a pair of corresponding sides?

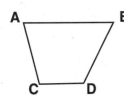 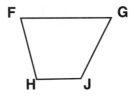

A AB and CD

B CD and HJ

C AC and GJ

D FG and FH

Read this passage, then answer questions 16 and 17.

The Monroes are building a fence around their yard. The yard is 52 feet wide and 64 feet long. The fence will be 5 feet high and will be made with boards that are 6 inches wide. There will be one gate in the fence, and it will be 4 feet wide.

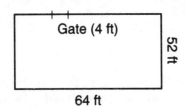

16 What is the total length of fence they must build, not counting the gate?

F 228 feet

G 16,640 feet

H 3328 feet

J 236 feet

17 The gate will be made out of the same kind of wood as the fence. How many boards will the Monroes need to build the gate? The boards are 10 feet long.

A 5

B 8

C 10

D 4

18 What will be the coordinates of point B if you move triangle ABC four units down?

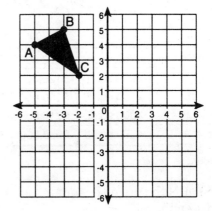

F (−7, 1)

G (−3, 5)

H (−3, 1)

J (−3, −5)

19 What fraction of 2 gallons is 10 pints?

A $\frac{1}{20}$

B $\frac{5}{8}$

C $\frac{5}{16}$

D $\frac{1}{5}$

20 For which of these equations would $a = 3$ when $b = 7$?

F $2a = b$

G $ab = 10$

H $2a + b = 15$

J $a^2 = b + 2$

21 If 5 workers can build 2 cars in an 8-hour shift, how long will it take 15 workers to build 36 cars?

A 48 hours

B 54 hours

C 6 hours

D 18 hours

147

GO

The chart below shows the area, price, and down payment for different houses. Use the graph to answer questions 22 through 25.

	Area	Price	Down Payment
First Choice	1700 sq. ft.	$102,000	$12,000
Family	2000 sq. ft.	$120,000	$14,000
Haven	2500 sq. ft.	$150,000	$16,000
Executive	3000 sq. ft.	$210,000	$25,000
Royal	4000 sq. ft.	$280,000	$30,000

22 What is the price per square foot of the Haven model?

F $80 per square foot

G $50 per square foot

H $25 per square foot

J   Not Given

23 What is the difference between the most and least expensive homes?

A $178,000

B $68,000

C $168,000

D $182,000

24 How much larger is the Executive model than the Haven model?

F   10%

G   20%

H   25%

J   30%

25 If you had $18,000 and wanted to buy the Royal home, how much more would you need to make the down payment?

A $12,000

B $30,000

C $22,000

D $8000

26 In the triangle below, angle MNO is a right angle. If angle MON equals 30°, what is the measure of angle NMO?

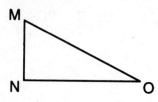

F   40°

G   45°

H   60°

J   70°

27 Woody wants to send 6 gifts to his family in Indiana. Each gift weighs $2\frac{1}{4}$ pounds. How much do the gifts weigh all together?

A $12\frac{1}{4}$

B $13\frac{1}{2}$

C $12\frac{1}{2}$

D $13\frac{1}{4}$

28 At a family reunion in the Southwest, there were 42 people from Colorado, 28 from New Mexico, 17 from Utah, and 3 from Arizona. If you began speaking to one of the people without knowing where the person was from, what are the chances the person would be from Colorado?

F   7 out of 15

G   21 out of 50

H   6 out of 15

J   21 out of 40

29 A standard paperback book is about —

A   10 in. by 12 in.

B   2 in. by 4 in.

C   8 in. by 16 in.

D   4 in. by 7 in.

STOP

Answer Keys

Reading
Unit 1,
Vocabulary
Lesson 1-pg. 12
A   C
B   F
1   A
2   J
3   B
4   H
5   D
6   F
7   B
8   H
Lesson 2-pg. 13
A   B
B   H
1   D
2   G
3   A
4   H
5   C
6   G
7   D
Lesson 3-pg. 14
A   C
B   F
1   B
2   F
3   D
4   H
5   D
6   H
7   A
8   G
Lesson 4-pg. 15
A   D
B   F
1   B
2   F
3   D
4   H
5   A
Lesson 5-pg. 16
A   B
B   J
1   B
2   F

3   C
4   J
5   A
6   H
Lesson 6-pg. 17
A   C
B   G
1   A
2   G
3   D
4   J
5   A
Lesson 7-pgs. 18-21
E1   D
E2   F
1   C
2   F
3   B
4   J
5   B
6   F
7   D
8   H
9   C
10   F
11   D
12   F
13   B
14   G
15   C
16   J
17   A
18   H
19   B
20   F
21   D
22   F
23   C
24   F
25   B
26   G
27   D
28   H
29   C
30   F
31   C
32   G
33   B

34   J
Unit 2, Reading
Comprehension
Lesson 8-pg. 22
A   D
1   C
2   J
3   A
Lesson 9-pgs. 23-26
A   B
1   B
2   F
3   D
4   H
5   D
6   H
7   A
8   H
9   A
10   J
11   B
12   J
13   B
Lesson 10-pgs. 27-32
A   B
1   D
2   G
3   A
4   G
5   C
6   H
7   A
8   G
9   D
10   F
11   B
12   H
13   A
14   J
15   B
16   F
17   C
18   G
19   D
20   F
21   B
22   J
Lesson 11-pgs. 33-41

E1   C
1   A
2   J
3   A
4   J
5   C
6   G
7   C
8   J
9   B
10   F
11   C
12   J
13   B
14   F
15   C
16   F
17   B
18   J
19   A
20   J
21   B
22   H
23   C
24   H
25   A
26   J
27   B
28   G
29   A
30   H
31   B
32   H
33   A
Unit 3, Test Practice
Part 1-pgs. 44-47
E1   D
E2   H
1   C
2   G
3   C
4   F
5   B
6   J
7   A
8   H
9   A
10   J

11	A
12	H
13	C
14	J
15	A
16	H
17	B
18	G
19	D
20	G
21	D
22	G
23	C
24	H
25	D
26	G
27	A
28	G
29	D
30	G
31	D
32	G
33	C
34	F

Test Practice
Part 2-pgs. 48-56

E1	C
1	A
2	J
3	C
4	G
5	D
6	F
7	D
8	H
9	C
10	F
11	D
12	G
13	B
14	J
15	C
16	F
17	C
18	F
19	D
20	F
21	C
22	J
23	B
24	H
25	A
26	J

27	A
28	H
29	A
30	J
31	B
32	F
33	D
34	G
35	C

Language
Unit 1, Language
Mechanics
Lesson 1-pgs. 58-59

A	A
B	J
1	B
2	J
3	A
4	H
5	B
6	F
7	B
8	F
9	D
10	H
11	C
12	F
13	D
14	J
15	B
16	H
17	A

Lesson 2-pgs. 60-62

A	C
B	J
1	A
2	H
3	D
4	G
5	C
6	J
7	B
8	F
9	D
10	H
11	B
12	J
13	A
14	H
15	B
16	F
17	C
18	J

19	A
20	G

Lesson 3-pgs. 63-66

E1	D
1	A
2	H
3	B
4	J
5	D
6	F
7	B
8	F
9	D
10	F
11	C
12	G
13	D
14	J
15	A
16	H
17	A
18	G
19	D
20	H
21	A
22	J
23	A
24	H
25	B
26	H
27	C
28	G
29	D

Unit 2, Language
Expression
Lesson 4-pgs. 67-69

A	A
B	J
1	C
2	G
3	A
4	J
5	B
6	F
7	D
8	G
9	C
10	F
11	C
12	H
13	B
14	F
15	D
16	H

17	D
18	G
19	C
20	F

Lesson 5-pgs. 70-72

A	A
B	H
C	D
1	A
2	H
3	B
4	H
5	B
6	J
7	C
8	F
9	D
10	G
11	B
12	J
13	A
14	J
15	A

Lesson 6-pgs. 73-76

A	B
1	A
2	H
3	D
4	G
5	D
6	F
7	D
8	H
9	A
10	G
11	B
12	G
13	D
14	F

Lesson 7-pgs. 77-80

E1	C
1	C
2	J
3	B
4	J
5	B
6	G
7	B
8	G
9	A
10	J
11	B
12	H

13	A
14	J
15	C
16	G
17	C
18	J
19	A
20	F

Unit 3, Spelling
Lesson 8-pgs. 81-82

A	D
B	G
1	A
2	H
3	B
4	G
5	C
6	J
7	A
8	H
9	C
10	F
11	E
12	H
13	B
14	H
15	A
16	H
17	D
18	F

Lesson 9-pgs. 83-84

E1	D
E2	H
1	A
2	G
3	D
4	J
5	B
6	H
7	A
8	F
9	D
10	H
11	D
12	H
13	A
14	J
15	C
16	F
17	A
18	G
19	B
20	J

Unit 4, Study Skills
Lesson 10-pgs. 85-86

A	B
1	C
2	F
3	C
4	F
5	C
6	J
7	A
8	G

Lesson 11-pgs. 87-89

E1	C
E2	F
1	C
2	F
3	D
4	J
5	D
6	G
7	A
8	H
9	B
10	J
11	C
12	F
13	C
14	G
15	B
16	F

Unit 5, Test Practice
Part 1-pgs. 92-94

E1	C
1	C
2	G
3	D
4	F
5	D
6	F
7	B
8	H
9	A
10	H
11	D
12	F
13	B
14	J
15	B
16	H
17	A
18	F
19	B
20	J

21	C

Test Practice
Part 2-pgs. 95-98

E1	D
1	D
2	G
3	B
4	J
5	B
6	H
7	B
8	G
9	A
10	J
11	C
12	H
13	A
14	H
15	D
16	G
17	D
18	H
19	B
20	F

Test Practice
Part 3-pgs. 99-100

E1	A
E2	J
1	B
2	H
3	A
4	F
5	D
6	G
7	C
8	F
9	D
10	H
11	E
12	H
13	A
14	G
15	A
16	J
17	B
18	F
19	C
20	F

Test Practice
Part 4-pgs. 101-102

E1	D
1	A
2	J
3	B

4	H
5	C
6	F
7	D
8	H
9	D
10	G
11	D

Math
Unit 1, Concepts
Lesson 1-pgs. 104-105

A	B
B	J
1	B
2	F
3	D
4	H
5	B
6	H
7	A
8	J
9	B
10	H
11	A
12	J
13	B
14	H
15	B

Lesson 2-pgs. 106-107

A	D
B	F
1	D
2	G
3	A
4	G
5	C
6	J
7	C
8	H
9	A
10	G
11	A
12	G
13	C

Lesson 3-pgs. 108-109

A	D
B	F
1	C
2	F
3	A
4	G
5	D
6	H

7	D	B	K	9	A	14	G
8	F	1	D	10	H	15	D
9	B	2	H	11	B	16	H
10	G	3	E	12	G	17	B
11	A	4	F	13	C	18	F
12	G	5	B	14	F	19	D
13	D	6	J	15	D	20	H

Lesson 4-pgs. 110-111 (col 1) / **Lesson 7-pgs. 116-117** (col 2) / **Lesson 9-pgs. 120-121** (col 3) / **Lesson 11-pgs. 126-127** (col 4)

Column 1

7 D
8 F
9 B
10 G
11 A
12 G
13 D
14 G
15 C

Lesson 4-pgs. 110-111

E1 A
E2 H
1 B
2 F
3 B
4 J
5 A
6 G
7 C
8 G
9 C
10 J
11 A
12 J
13 A
14 H
15 B
16 H

Unit 2, Computation
Lesson 5-pgs. 112-113

A E
B G
1 B
2 J
3 C
4 F
5 E
6 F
7 C
8 G
9 C
10 G
11 E
12 F
13 D
14 H
15 D
16 G
17 A
18 F

Lesson 6-pgs. 114-115

A C

Column 2

B K
1 D
2 H
3 E
4 F
5 B
6 J
7 A
8 G
9 E
10 G
11 C
12 F
13 D
14 G
15 C
16 J
17 E
18 F
19 D

Lesson 7-pgs. 116-117

A C
B K
1 A
2 J
3 E
4 G
5 C
6 F
7 D
8 G
9 C
10 J
11 A
12 G
13 E
14 J
15 B
16 H
17 A
18 K
19 D

Lesson 8-pgs. 118-119

A D
B F
1 B
2 H
3 A
4 J
5 B
6 H
7 B
8 F

Column 3

9 A
10 H
11 B
12 G
13 C
14 F
15 D
16 F
17 C
18 J
19 C
20 G

Lesson 9-pgs. 120-121

E1 E
E2 F
1 D
2 F
3 E
4 G
5 D
6 K
7 B
8 F
9 D
10 F
11 A
12 G
13 E
14 J
15 B
16 H
17 E
18 G
19 D
20 F
21 D
22 H

Unit 3, Applications
Lesson 10-pgs. 122-125

A D
1 D
2 F
3 C
4 G
5 C
6 F
7 D
8 G
9 B
10 H
11 D
12 H
13 A

Column 4

14 G
15 D
16 H
17 B
18 F
19 D
20 H

Lesson 11-pgs. 126-127

A C
1 A
2 H
3 B
4 J
5 C
6 J
7 A
8 J
9 B
10 H
11 A
12 G
13 D
14 H

Lesson 12-pgs. 128-131

A B
B J
1 D
2 G
3 A
4 G
5 D
6 G
7 A
8 J
9 C
10 G
11 C
12 J
13 A
14 H
15 B
16 J
17 C
18 F
19 B
20 F
21 D
22 G
23 A
24 G

Lesson 13-pgs. 132-133		E2	H	14	F
A	A	1	B	15	B
B	H	2	F	16	J
1	B	3	D	17	C
2	J	4	H	18	F
3	A	5	B	19	C
4	H	6	H	20	K
5	A	7	C	21	B
6	G	8	J	22	J
7	D	9	A		
8	H	10	G	**Test Practice**	
9	C	11	A	**Part 3-pgs. 145-148**	
10	J	12	F	E1	A
11	A	13	D	E2	J
12	G	14	H	1	D
Lesson 14-pgs. 134-137		15	B	2	G
E1	D	16	H	3	C
E2	F	17	D	4	F
1	A	18	F	5	D
2	J	19	B	6	H
3	B	20	H	7	C
4	J	21	B	8	J
5	C	22	G	9	C
6	G	23	D	10	F
7	A	24	F	11	B
8	J	25	C	12	J
9	C	26	G	13	B
10	J	**Test Practice**		14	H
11	B	**Part 2-pgs. 143-144**		15	B
12	J	E1	E	16	F
13	D	E2	G	17	D
14	F	1	E	18	H
15	D	2	G	19	B
16	H	3	C	20	J
17	B	4	J	21	A
18	G	5	A	22	J
19	C	6	K	23	A
20	G	7	A	24	G
21	D	8	G	25	A
22	F	9	C	26	H
23	D	10	J	27	B
24	H	11	C	28	F
Unit 4, Test Practice		12	K	29	D
Part 1-pgs. 140-142		13	D		
E1	A				

Reading Progress Chart

Circle your score for each lesson. Connect your scores to see how well you are doing.

Unit 1

Lesson 1	Lesson 2	Lesson 3	Lesson 4	Lesson 5	Lesson 6	Lesson 7	Lesson 8
8	7	8	5	6	5	34	3
7	6	7	4	5	4	33, 32, 31, 30, 29, 28, 27, 26	
6	5	6	3	4	3	25, 24, 23, 22	2
5	4	5	2	3	2	21, 20, 19, 18, 17, 16, 15, 14, 13, 12, 11, 10	
4	3	4	1	2	1	9, 8, 7, 6, 5, 4, 3, 2	1
3	2	3		1		1	
2	1	2					
1		1					

Unit 2

Lesson 9	Lesson 10	Lesson 11
13	22	33
12	21	32
11	20	31
10	19	30
9	18	29
8	17	28
7	16	27
6	15	26
5	14	25
4	13	24
3	12	23
2	11	22
1	10	21
	9	20
	8	19
	7	18
	6	17
	5	16
	4	15
	3	14
	2	13
	1	12
		11
		10
		9
		8
		7
		6
		5
		4
		3
		2
		1

Language Progress Chart

Circle your score for each lesson. Connect your scores to see how well you are doing.

Unit 1			Unit 2				Unit 3		Unit 4	
Lesson 1	Lesson 2	Lesson 3	Lesson 4	Lesson 5	Lesson 6	Lesson 7	Lesson 8	Lesson 9	Lesson 10	Lesson 11
17	20	29	20	15	14	20	18	20	8	16
16	19	28	19	14	13	19	17	19		15
15	18	27	18	13	12	18	16	18	7	14
14	17	26	17	12	11	17	15	17		13
13	16	25	16	11	10	16	14	16	6	12
12	15	24	15	10	9	15	13	15		11
11	14	23	14	9	8	14	12	14	5	10
10	13	22	13	8	7	13	11	13		9
9	12	21	12	7	6	12	10	12	4	8
8	11	20	11	6	5	11	9	11		7
7	10	19	10	5	4	10	8	10	3	6
6	9	18	9	4	3	9	7	9		5
5	8	17	8	3	2	8	6	8	2	4
4	7	16	7	2	1	7	5	7		3
3	6	15	6	1		6	4	6	1	2
2	5	14	5			5	3	5		1
1	4	13	4			4	2	4		
	3	12	3			3	1	3		
	2	11	2			2		2		
	1	10	1			1		1		
		9								
		8								
		7								
		6								
		5								
		4								
		3								
		2								
		1								

Math Progress Chart

Circle your score for each lesson. Connect your scores to see how well you are doing.

Unit 1

Lesson 1	Lesson 2	Lesson 3	Lesson 4
15	13	15	16
14	12	14	15
13	11	13	14
12	10	12	13
11	9	11	12
10	8	10	11
9	7	9	10
8	6	8	9
7	5	7	8
6	4	6	7
5	3	5	6
4	2	4	5
3	1	3	4
2		2	3
1		1	2
			1

Unit 2

Lesson 5	Lesson 6	Lesson 7	Lesson 8	Lesson 9
18	19	19	20	22
17	18	18	19	21
16	17	17	18	20
15	16	16	17	19
14	15	15	16	18
13	14	14	15	17
12	13	13	14	16
11	12	12	13	15
10	11	11	12	14
9	10	10	11	13
8	9	9	10	12
7	8	8	9	11
6	7	7	8	10
5	6	6	7	9
4	5	5	6	8
3	4	4	5	7
2	3	3	4	6
1	2	2	3	5
	1	1	2	4
			1	3
				2
				1

Unit 3

Lesson 10	Lesson 11	Lesson 12	Lesson 13	Lesson 14
20	14	24	12	24
19	13	23	11	23
18	12	22	10	22
17	11	21	9	21
16	10	20	8	20
15	9	19	7	19
14	8	18	6	18
13	7	17	5	17
12	6	16	4	16
11	5	15	3	15
10	4	14	2	14
9	3	13	1	13
8	2	12		12
7	1	11		11
6		10		10
5		9		9
4		8		8
3		7		7
2		6		6
1		5		5
		4		4
		3		3
		2		2
		1		1